I0492881

Color
Into Your
Life!

An Adult Coloring Book
To Inspire You!

Alice Langholt

Copyright © 2016 Alice Langholt

All rights reserved.
ISBN: 1532945434
ISBN-13: 978-1532945434

HOW TO USE THIS BOOK

Take a few slow, deep breaths. Invite in your creative, playful spirit!

Have your favorite art materials around you. The choices are all yours. Markers, colored pencils, gel pens, water colors, or whatever you like. Use a combination! There are no wrong answers here. Just let it flow!

Choose the word that inspires you and make it vibrate with your very own decorative touch. Play some music you like, and really enjoy this time.

As you fill the specially-chosen, inspirational words on the page with color, you engage the energy of those words, and you manifest more of that quality into your life. When the page is finished, be open to noticing the ways that quality begins flowing into your daily experiences.

The quotes on the facing pages are there to offer you some deeper ways to invite the words to play with you.

The process of coloring is found to be as beneficial and relaxing as meditation. Enjoy the activity and the results! Notice how you feel when you're done.

No time to do the whole page? No worries! It will be there when you're ready to continue.

It's time to begin.

Live Love, for that is your true essence living as you.

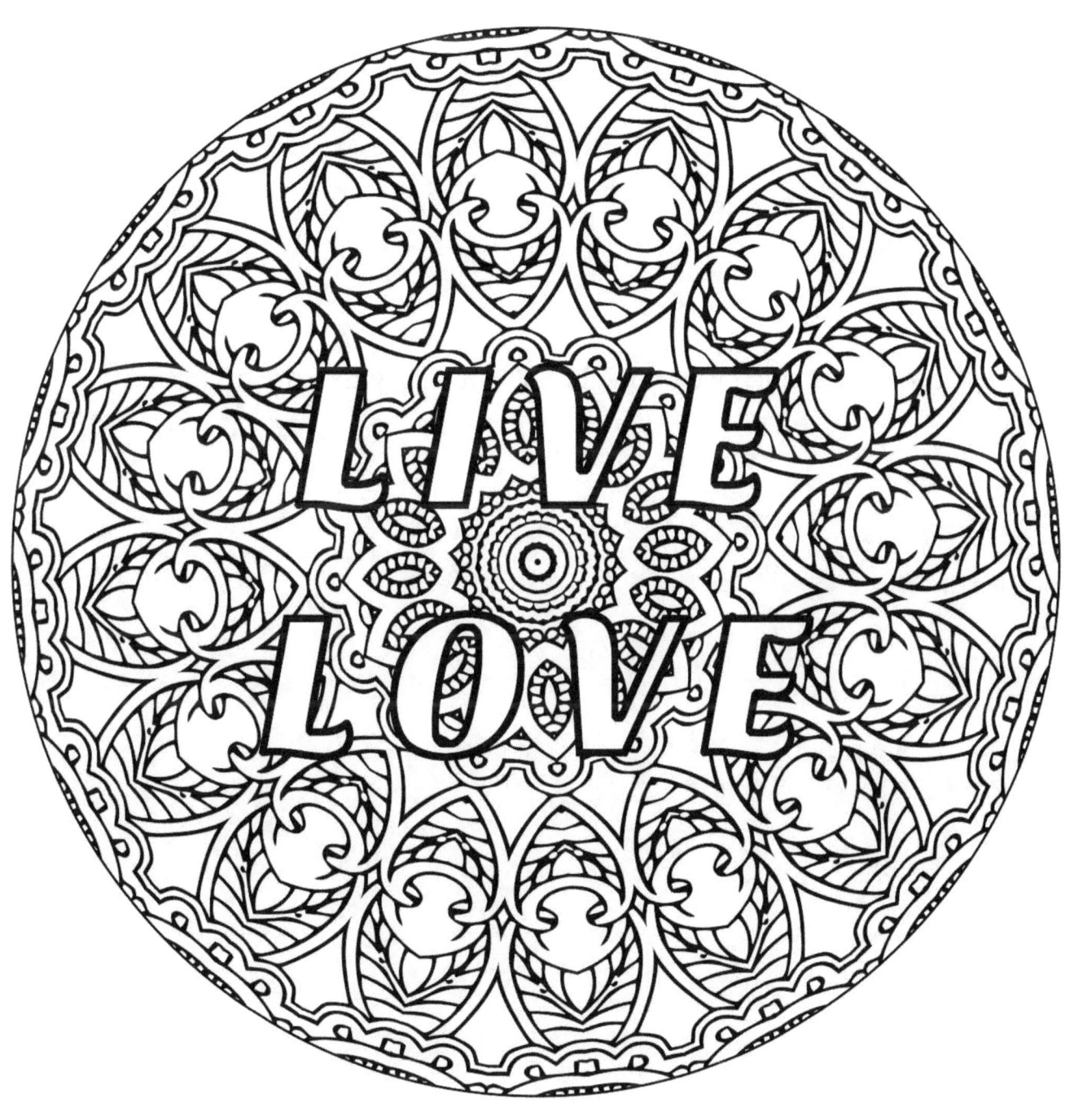

Peace comes when we know that it's always within, ready for us.

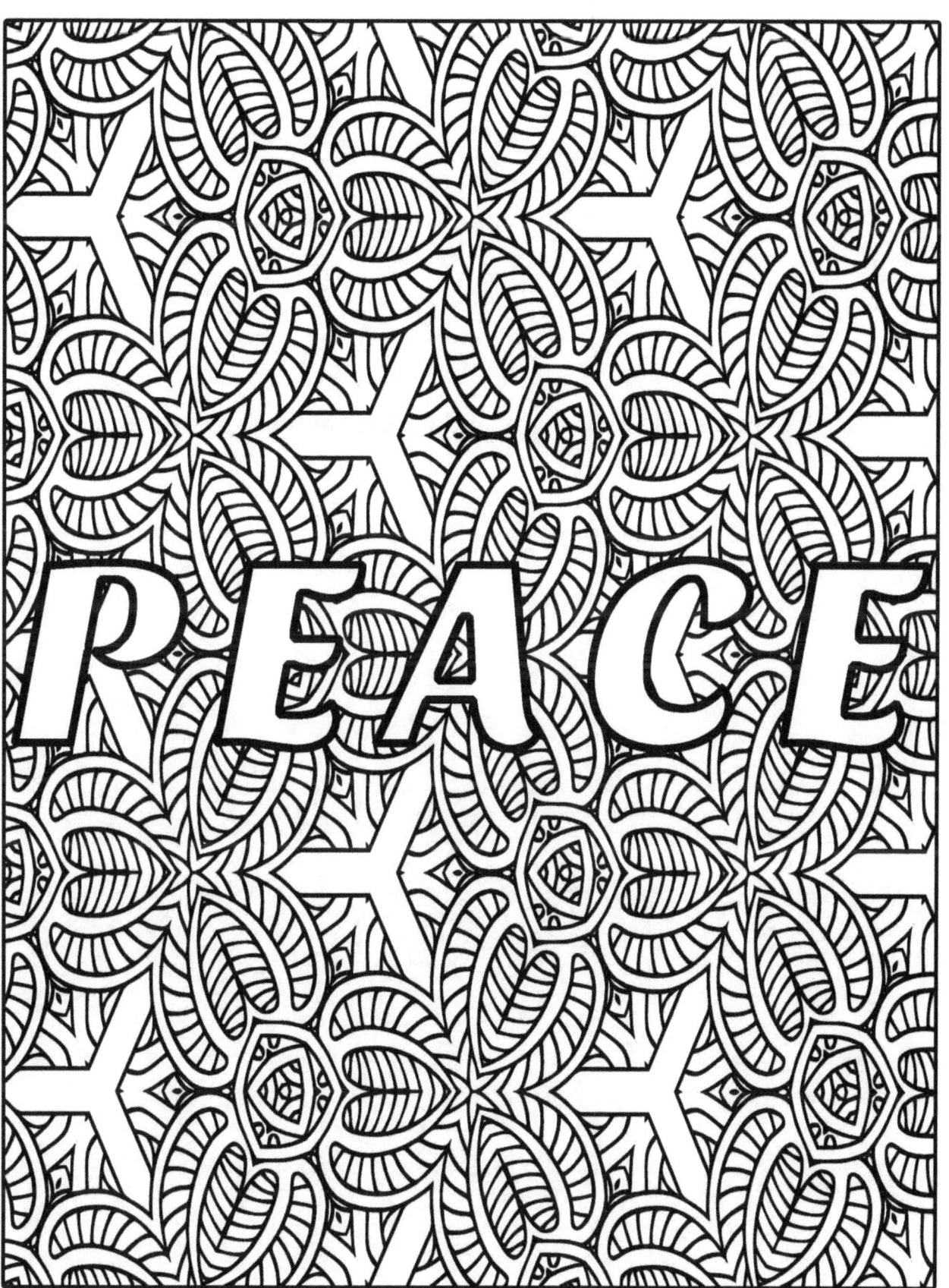

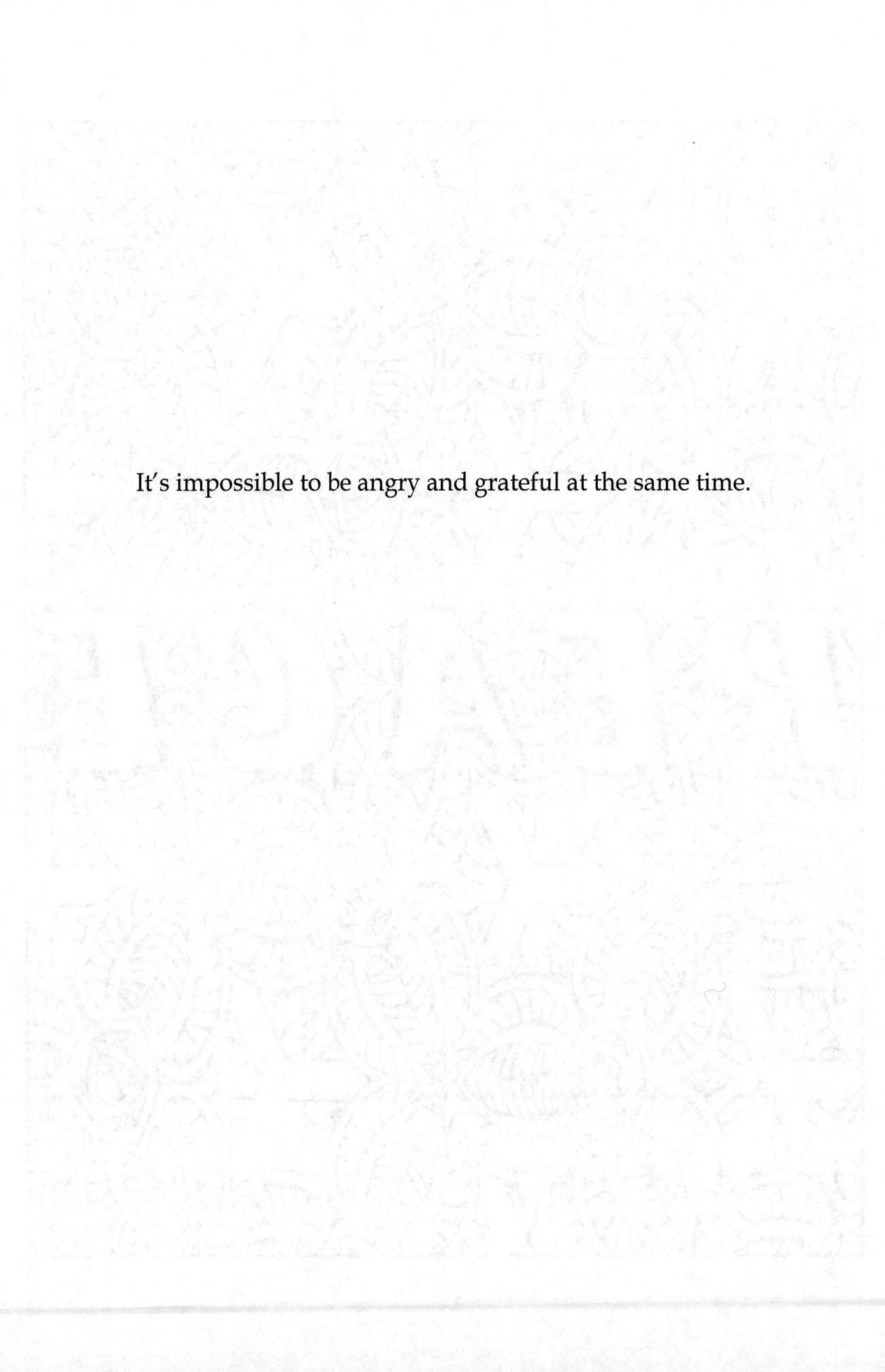

It's impossible to be angry and grateful at the same time.

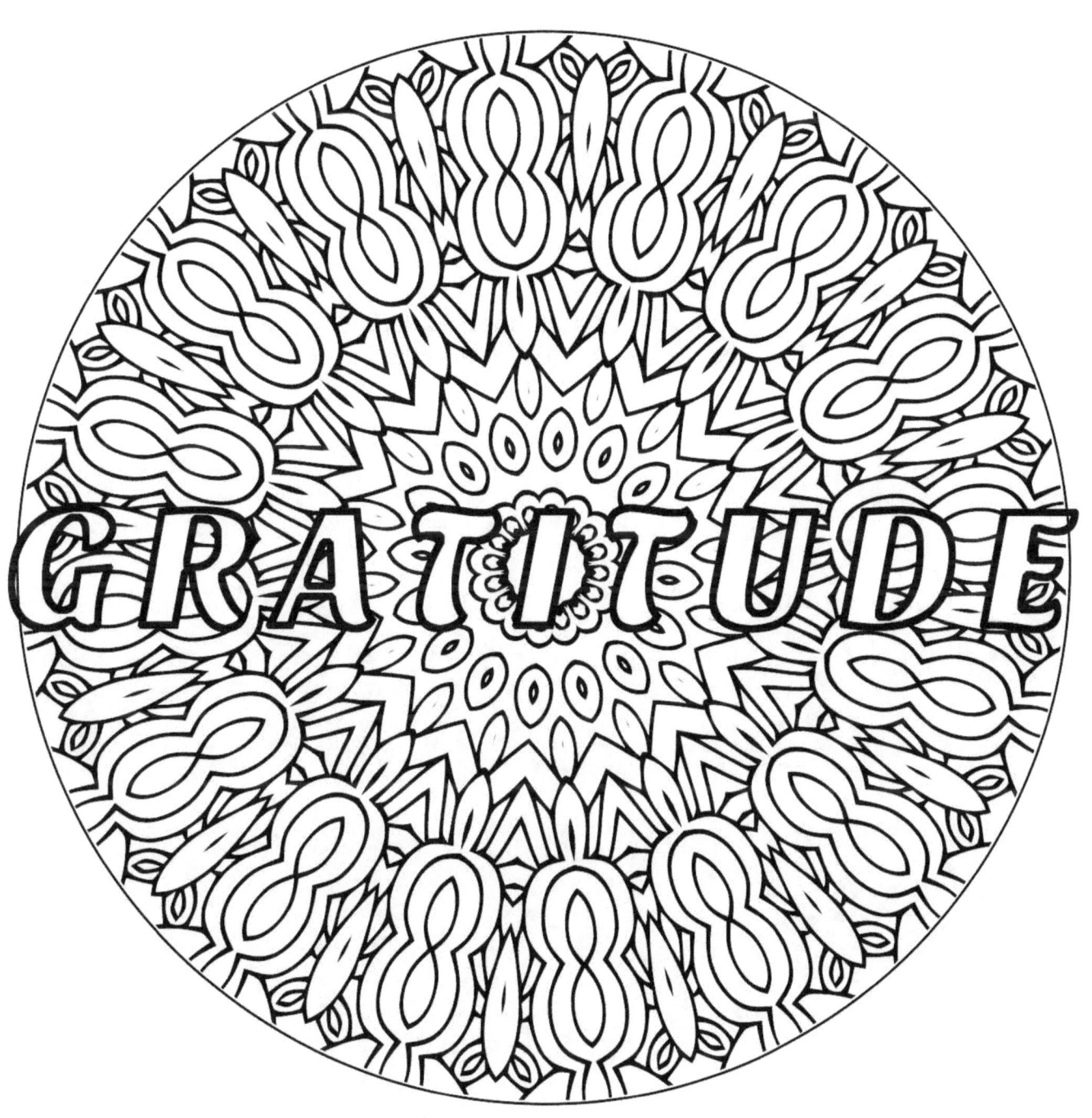

Happiness and gratitude are attached.
Notice one, and the other is there.

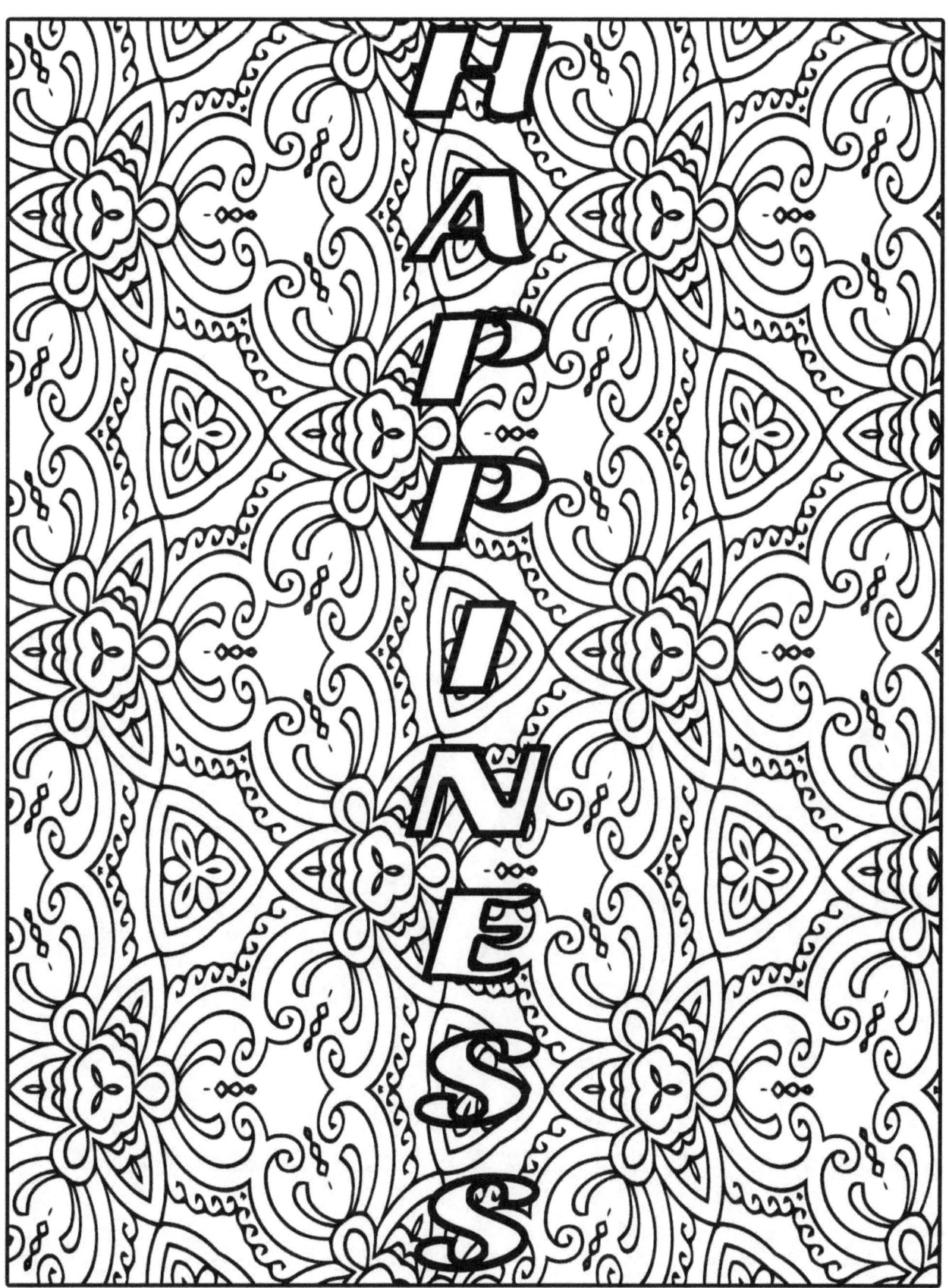

Compassion is seeing the oneness of all through the eyes of love.

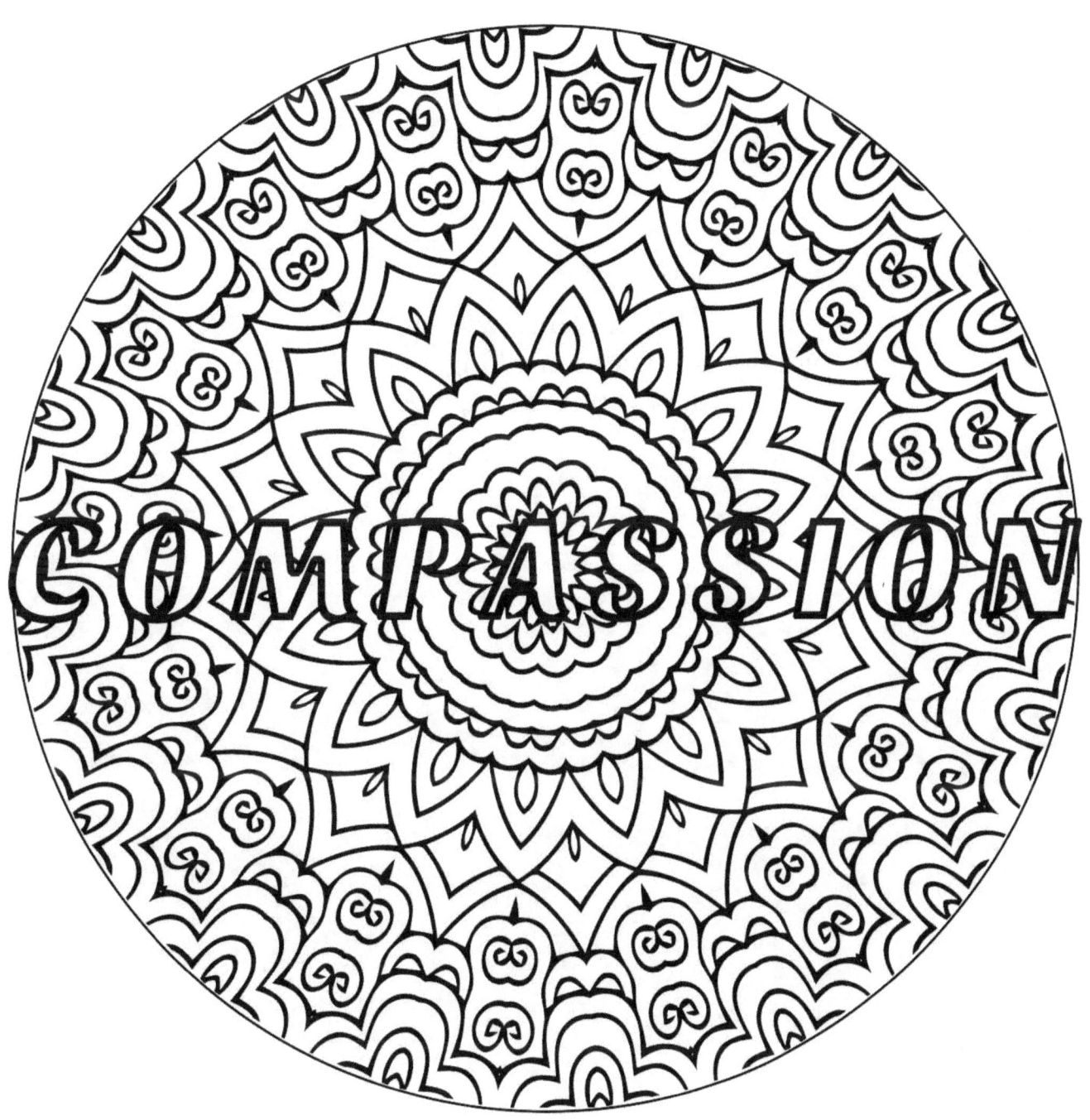

When you go within,
you connect with something much bigger
than you ever imagined.

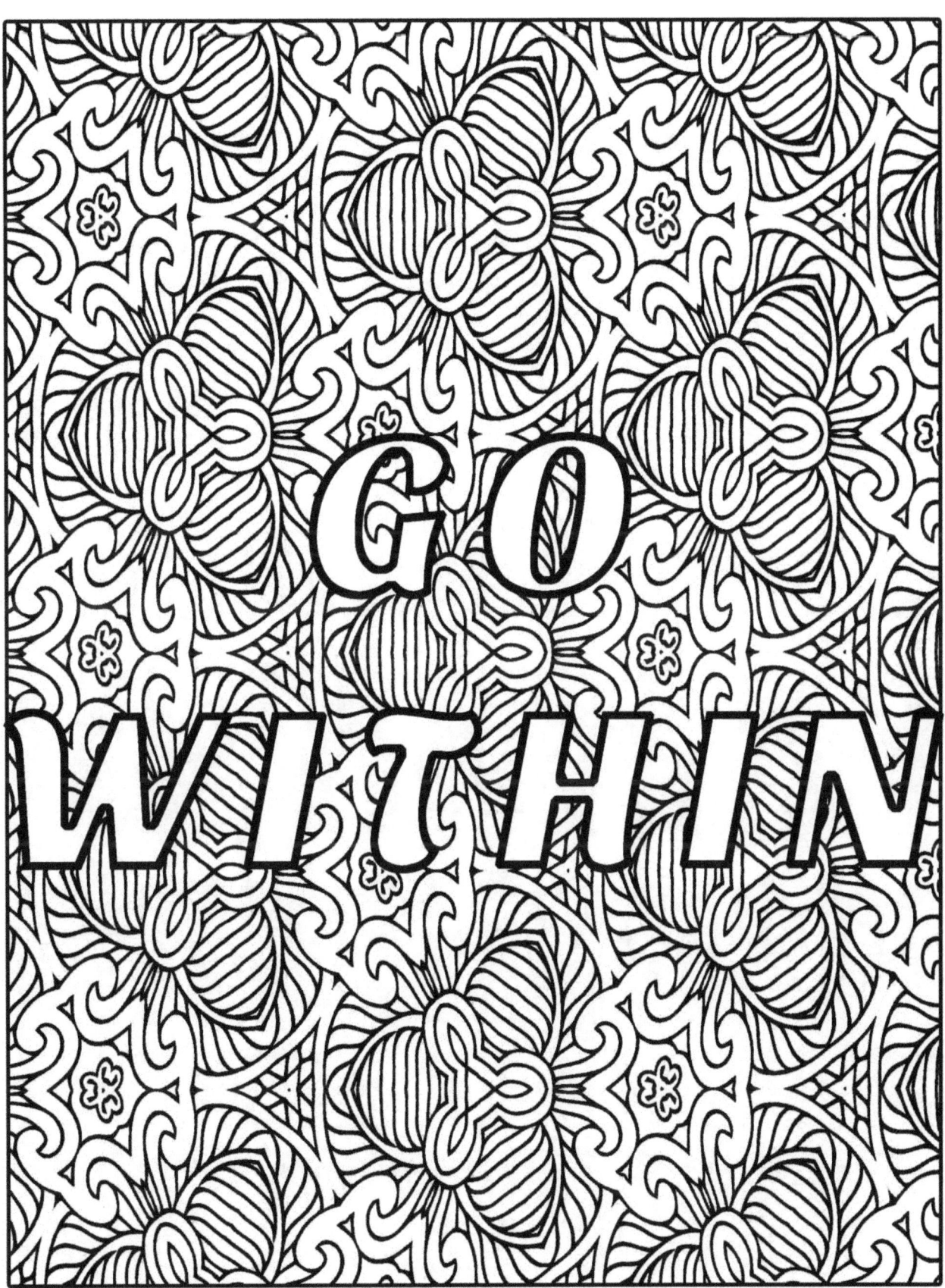

What you believe
becomes your reality.

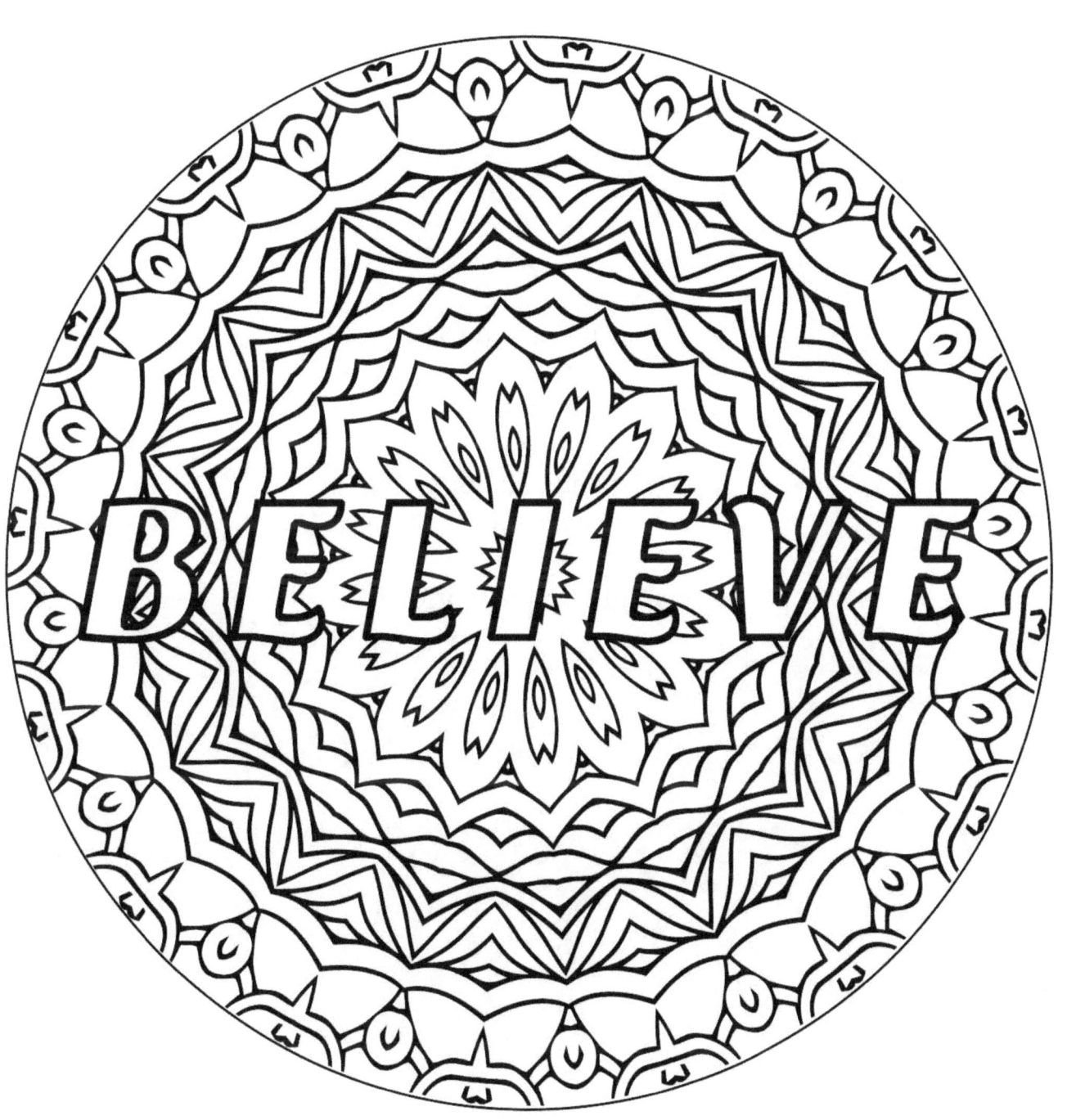

Bring goodness
into your
thoughts,
words,
and actions
each day.

Light up the world.

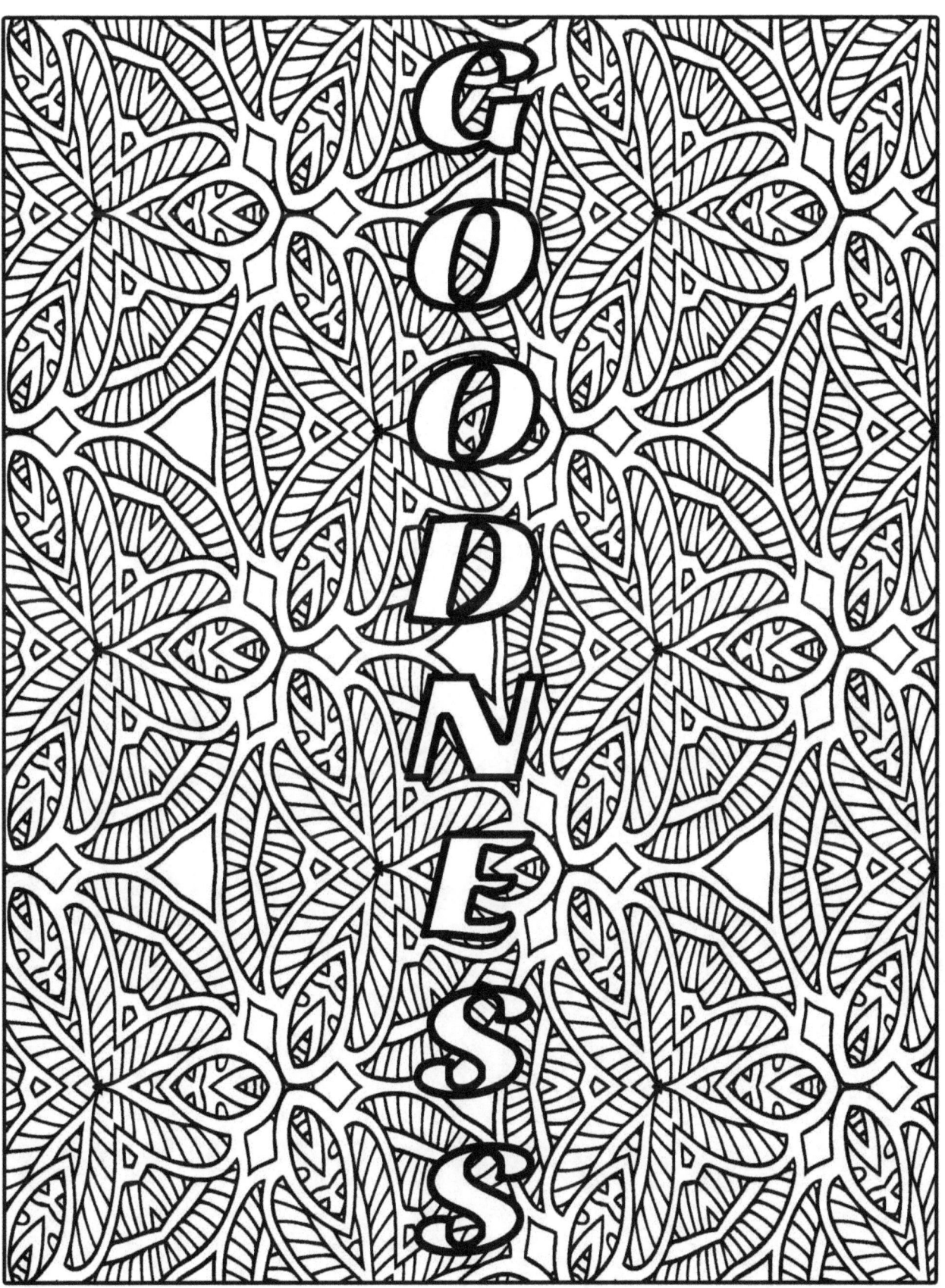

The heart
is the mind
of the soul.

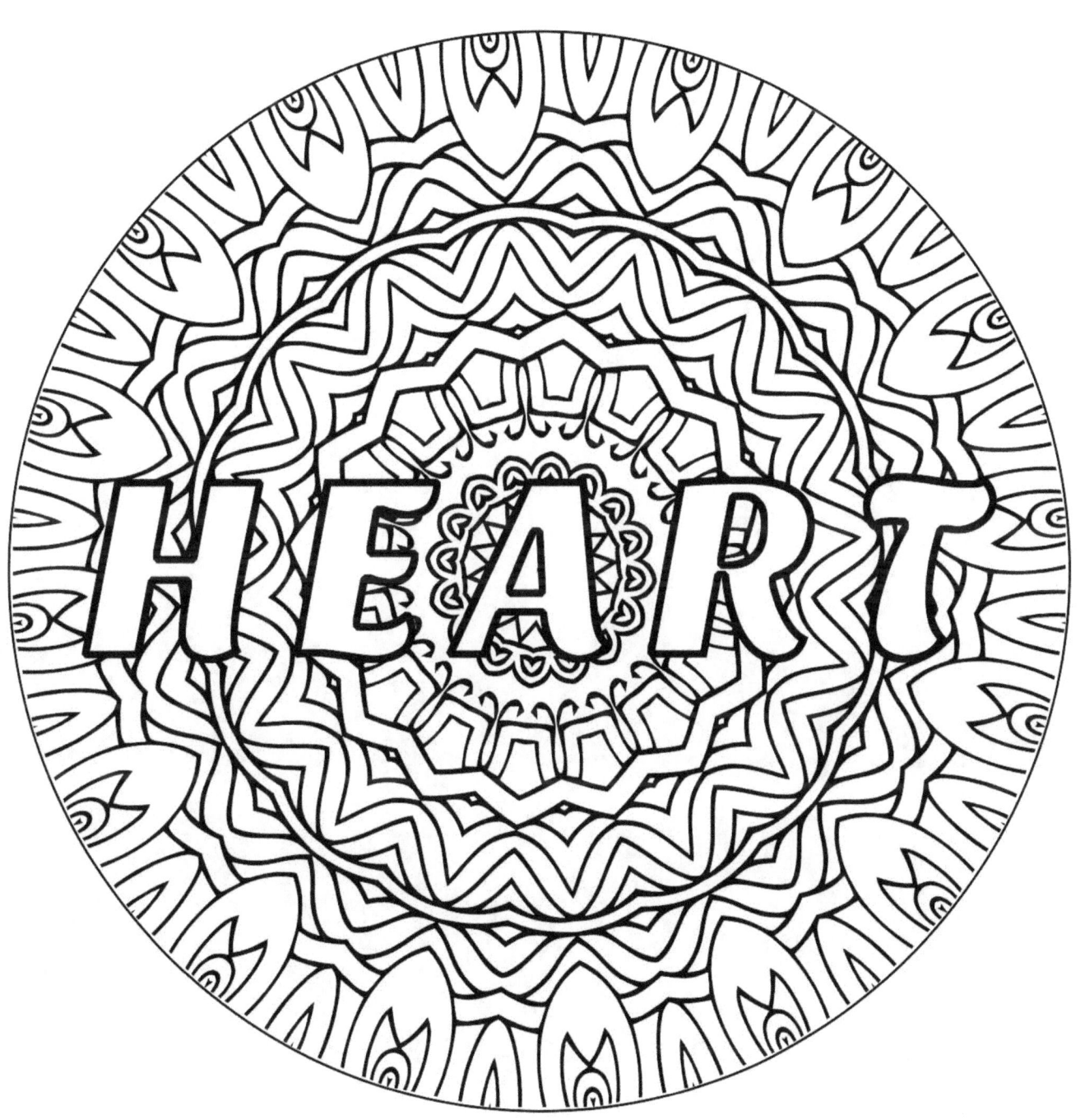

Free your mind.
The rest will follow.

You are beautiful
and so important.

And so it is.

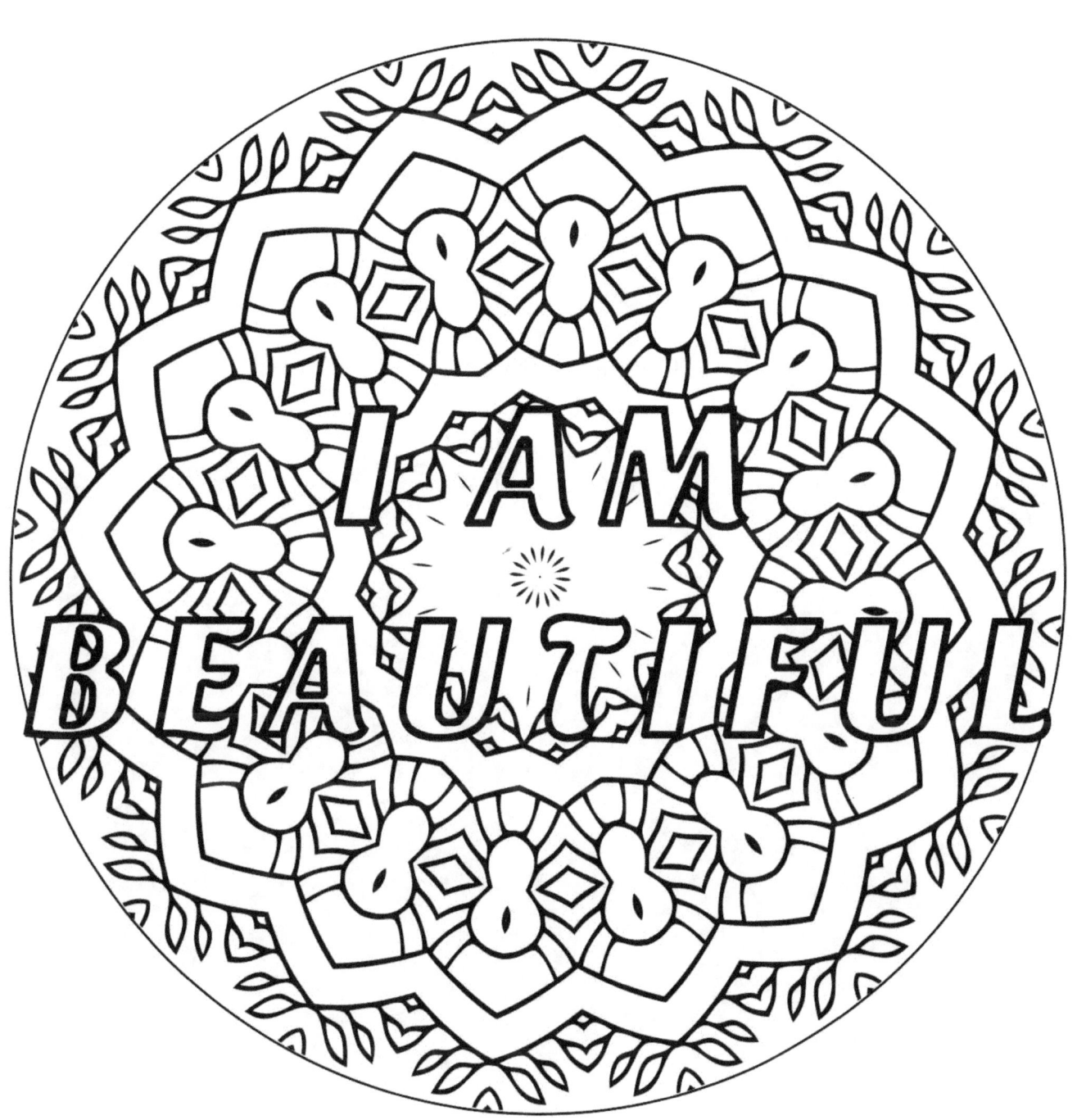

Connect with nature,
and its harmony
will resonate
into your being.

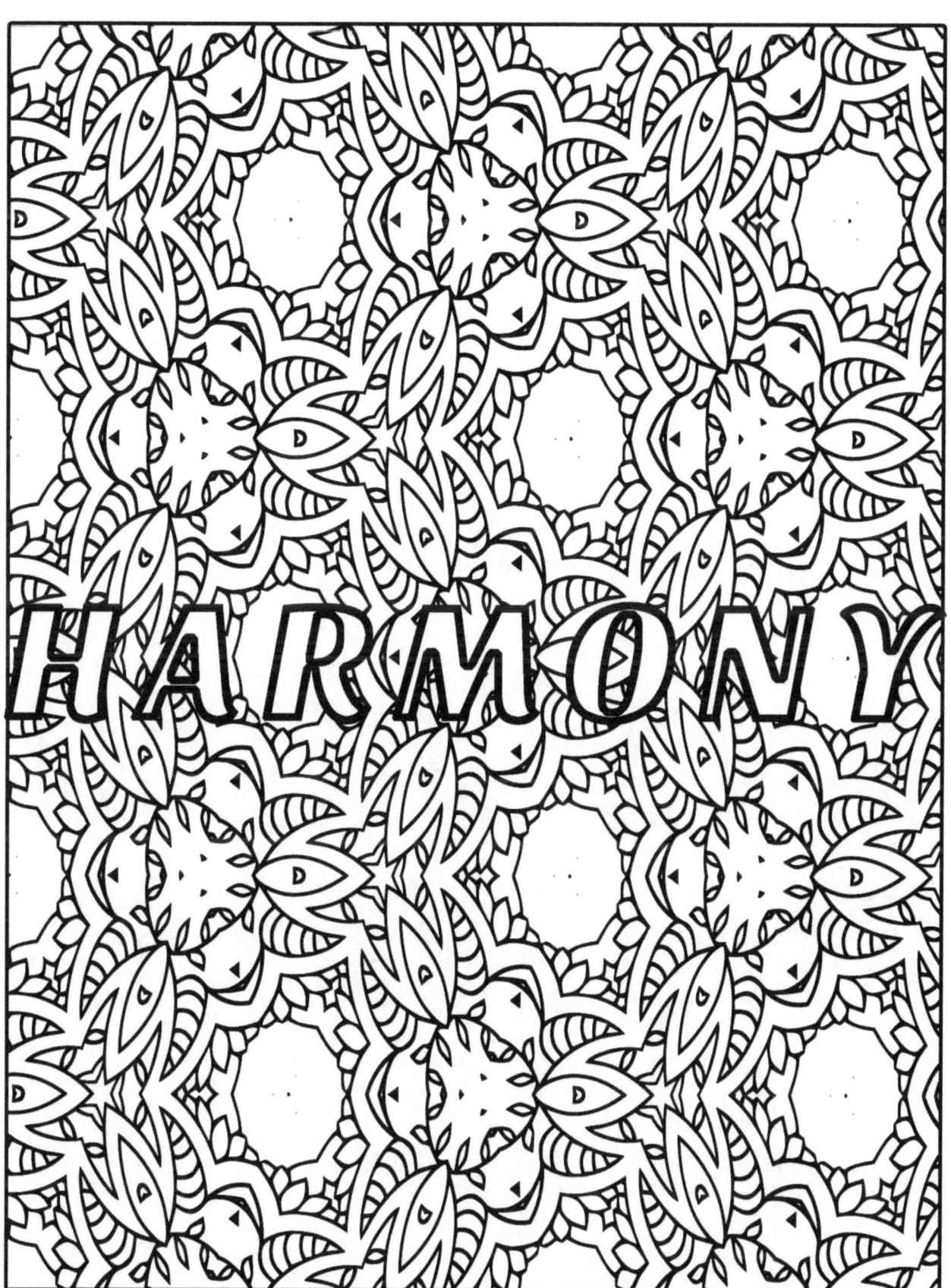

You express your unique essence
through creativity.
Creativity is
your life's true path.

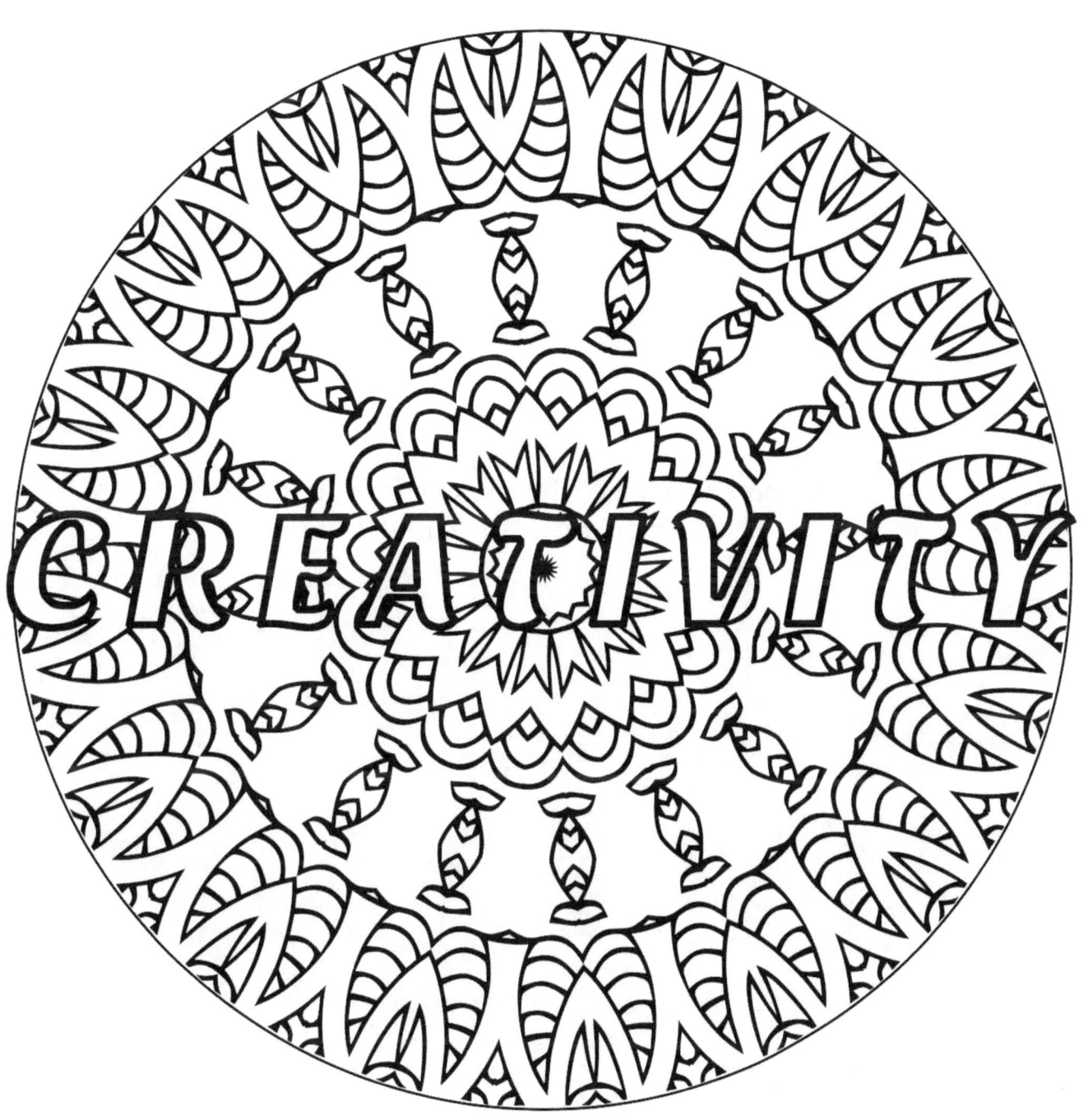

The more you notice the blessings in your life,
the more there are to find.

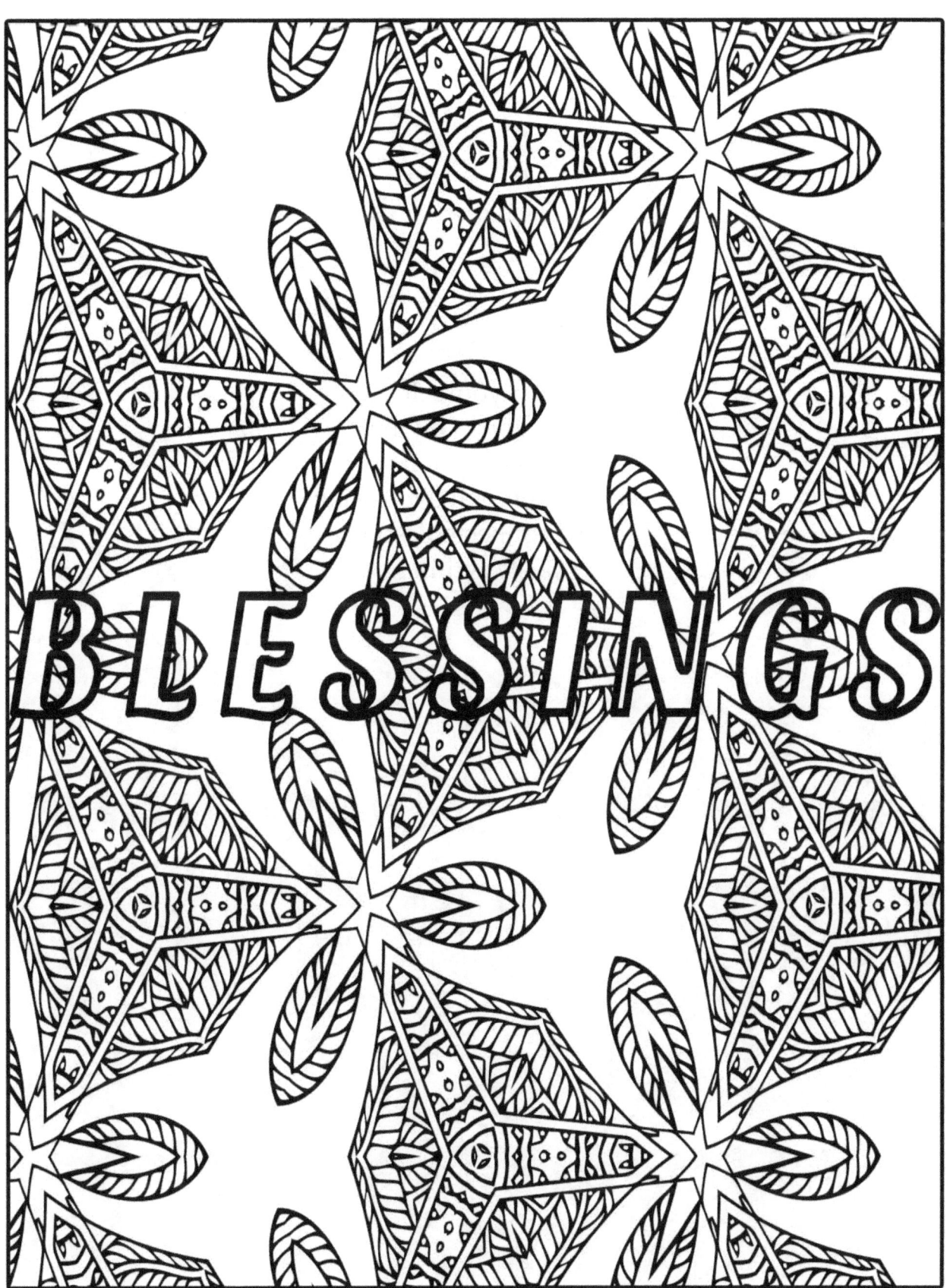

See yourself
in everyone you meet,
because all life
is an individual expression
of the connected essence
of everything.

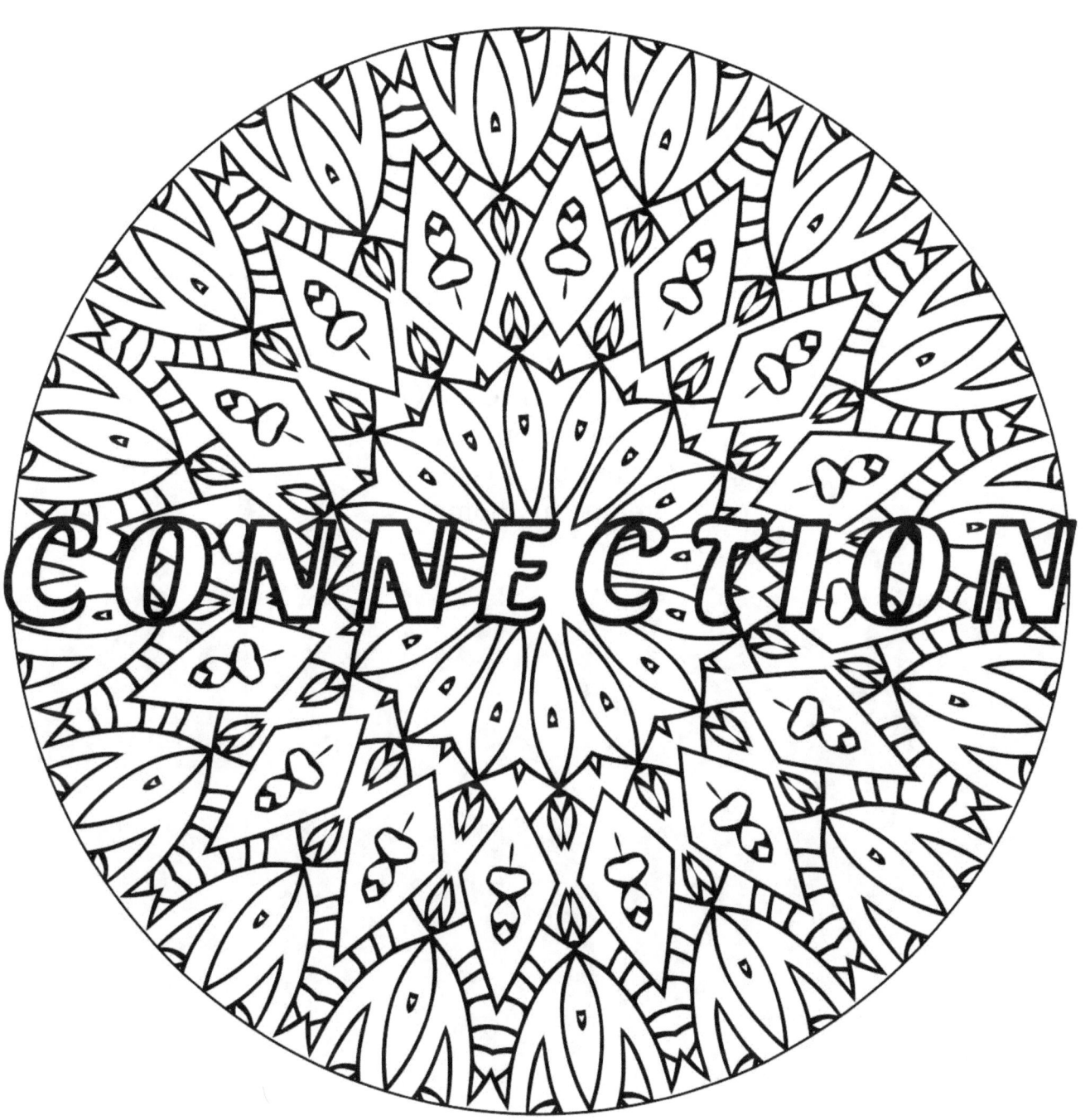

The true essence of YOU
is your Spirit.
Your body is its
temporary home.

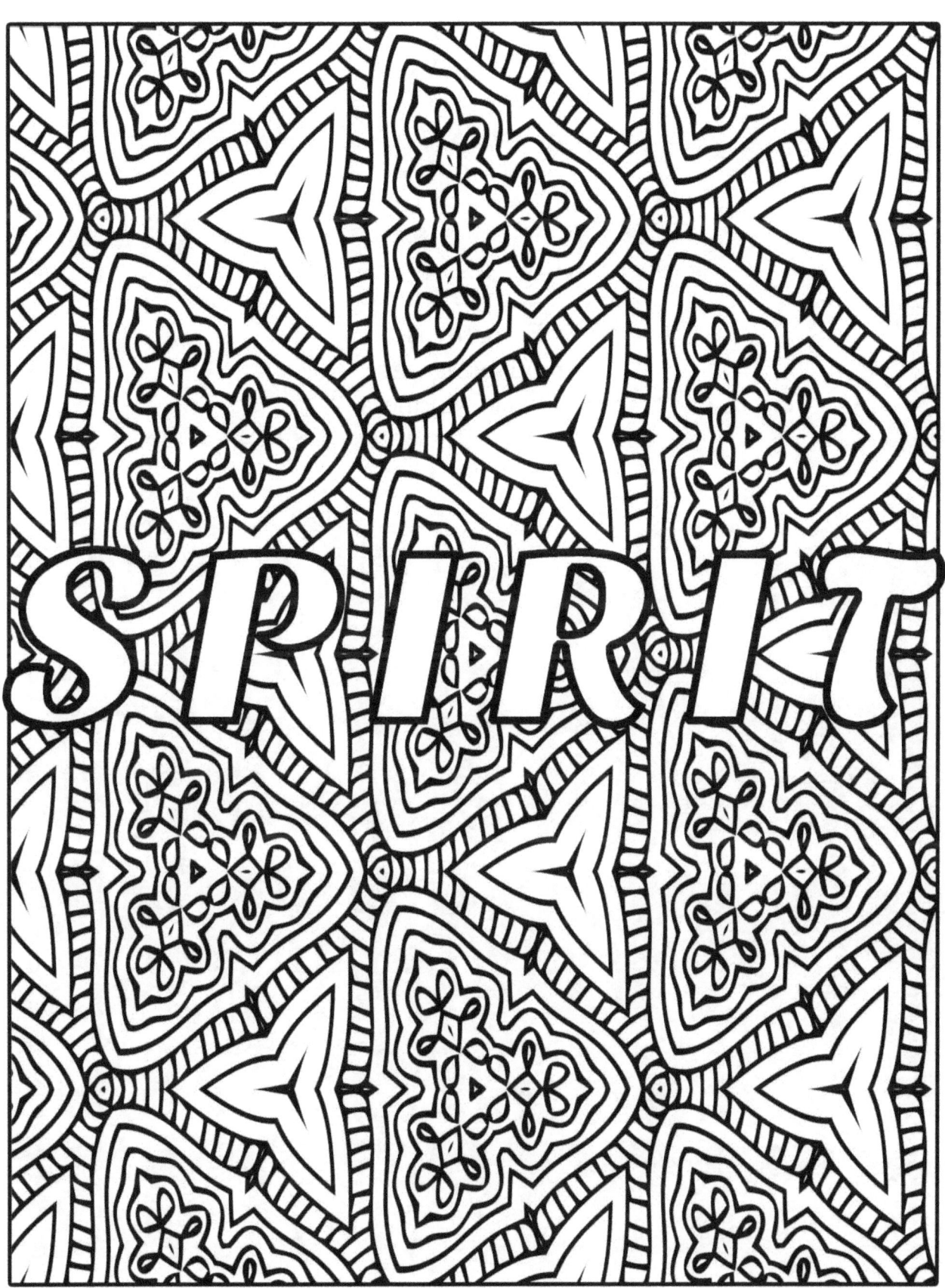

Empathy is
a motivating force
for acts of kindness.

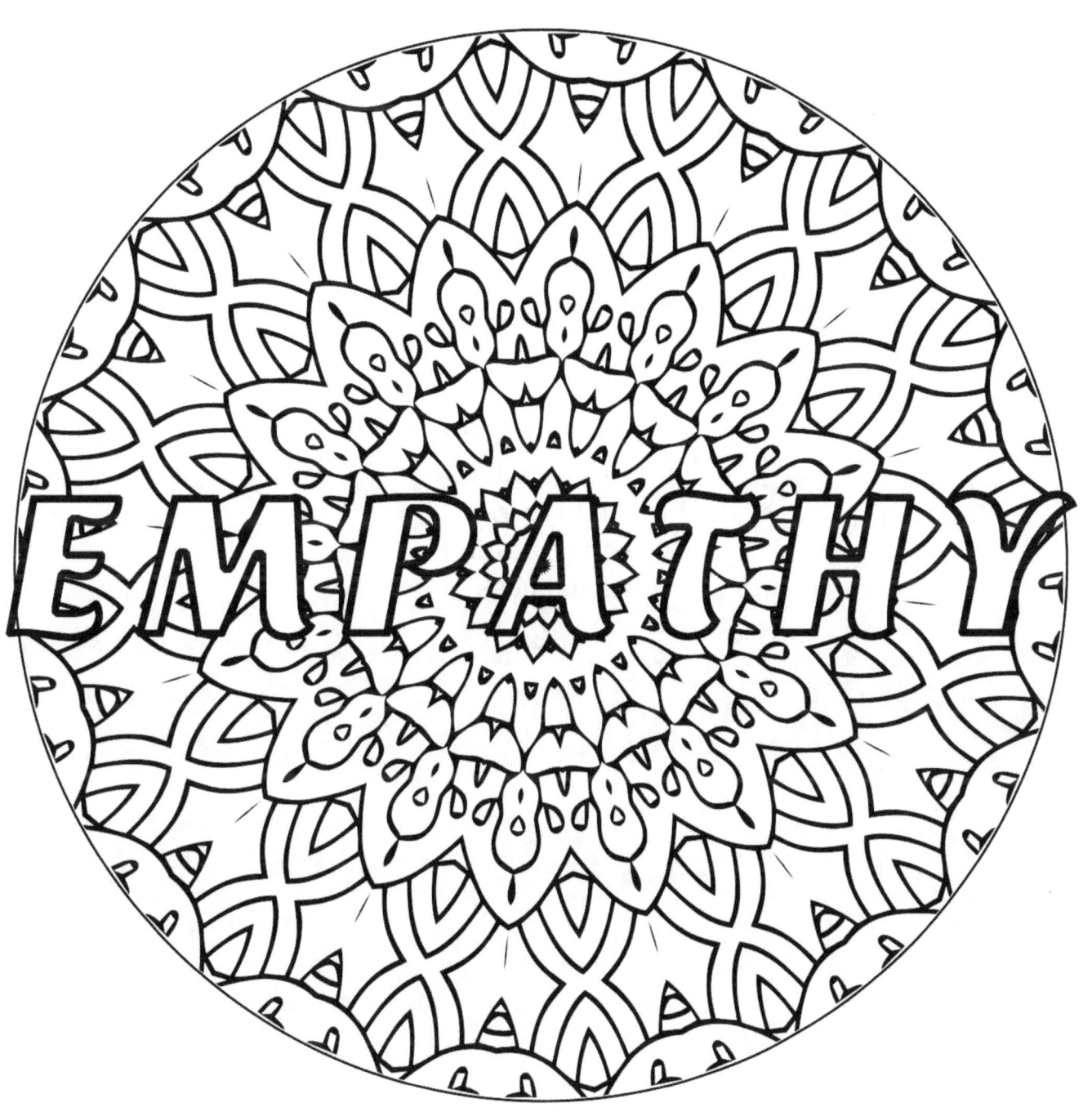

Balance in body,
mind, emotions
and spirit
is an indication
of vital health.

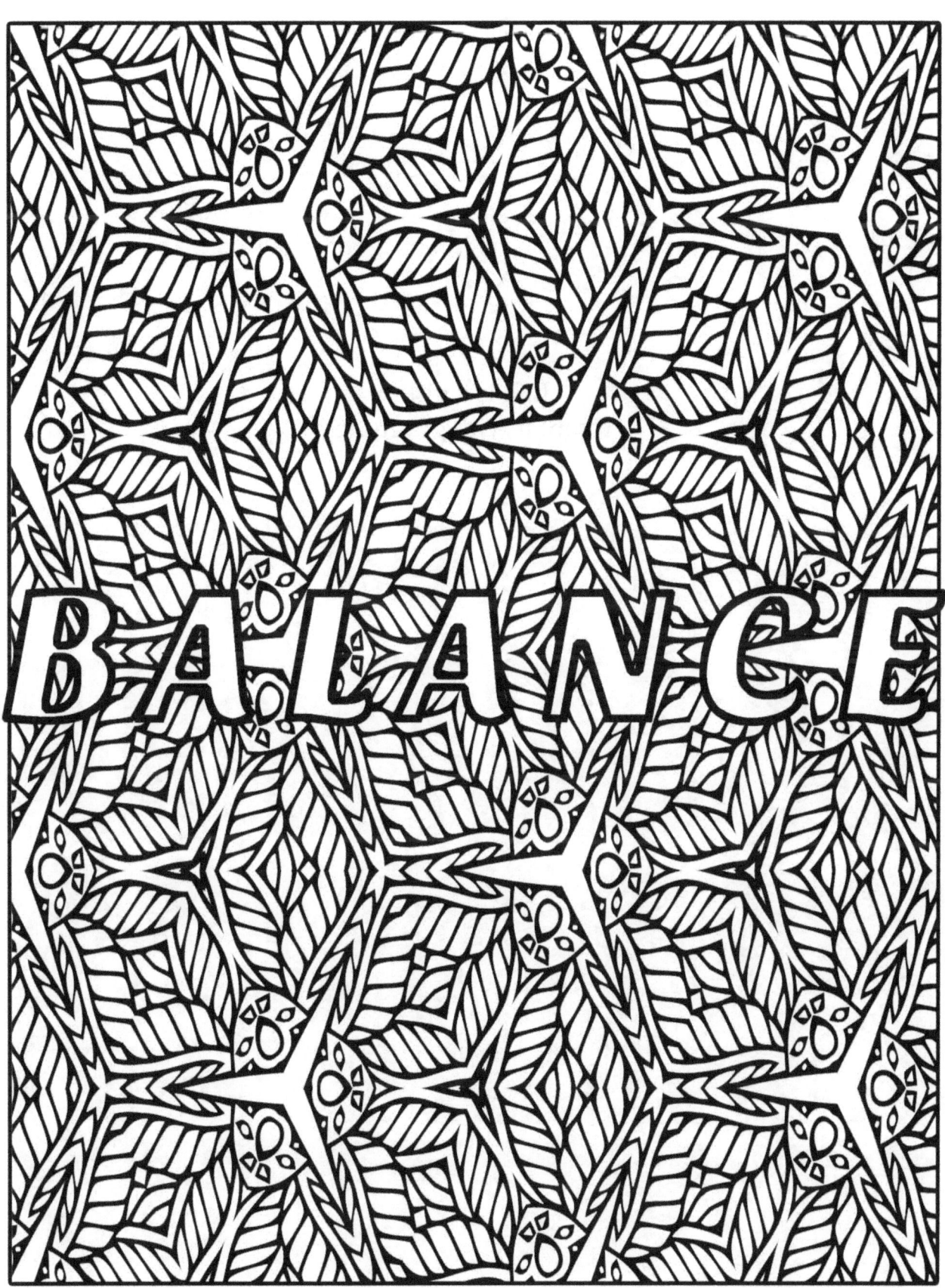

Life is a gift.
Accept it with gratitude.

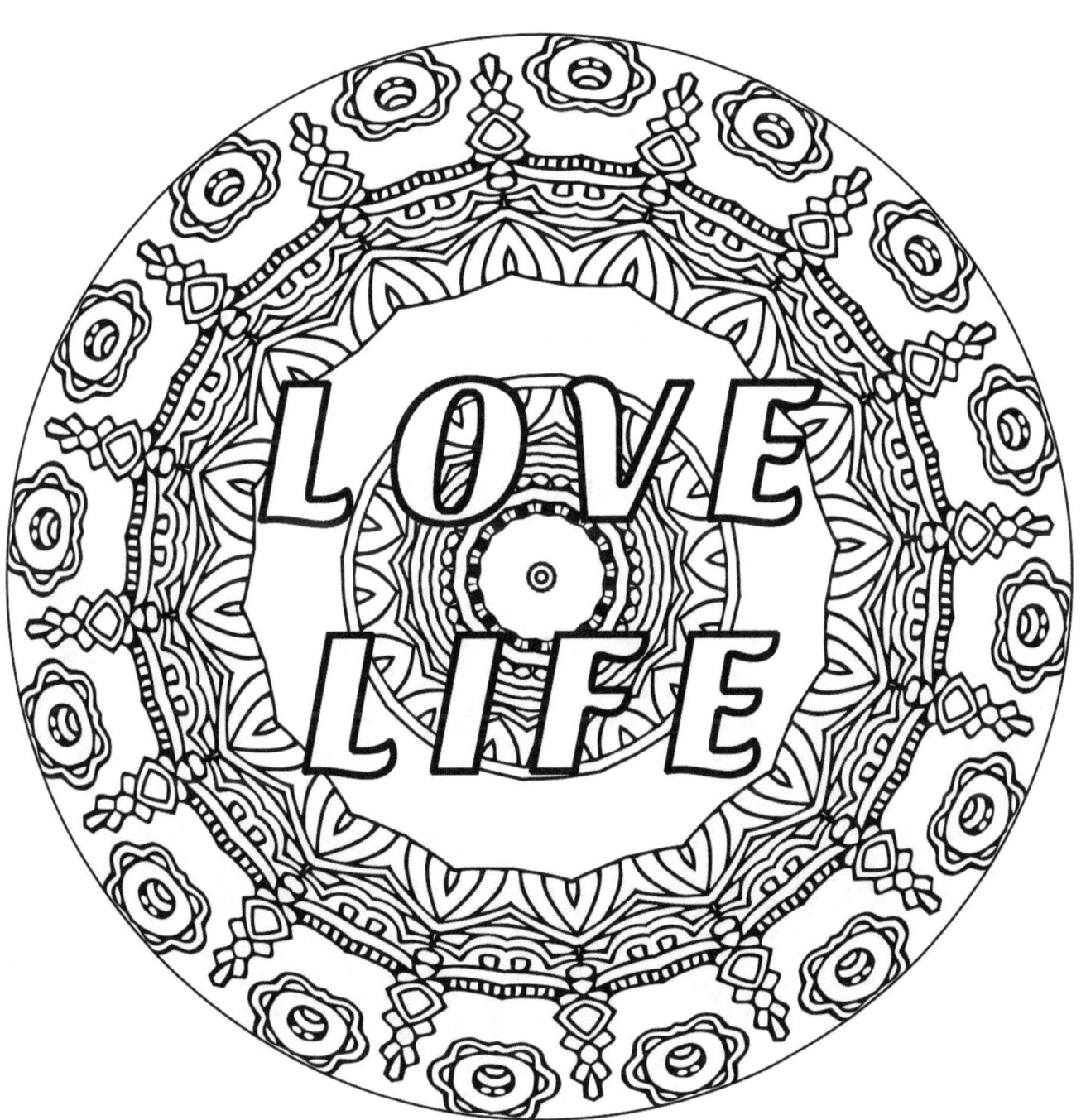

When we focus on
positive words,
and thoughts,
we feel positive
about life.

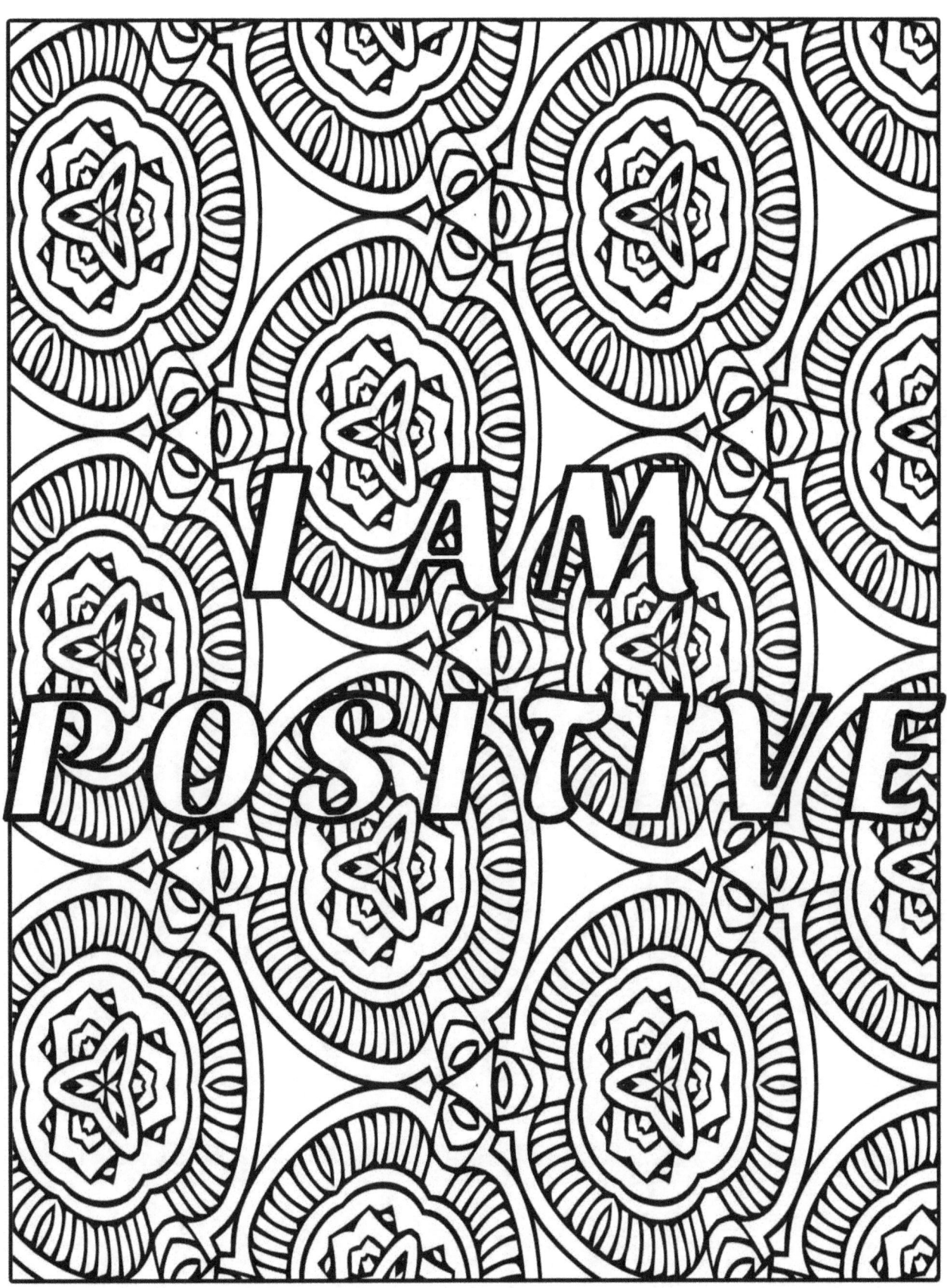

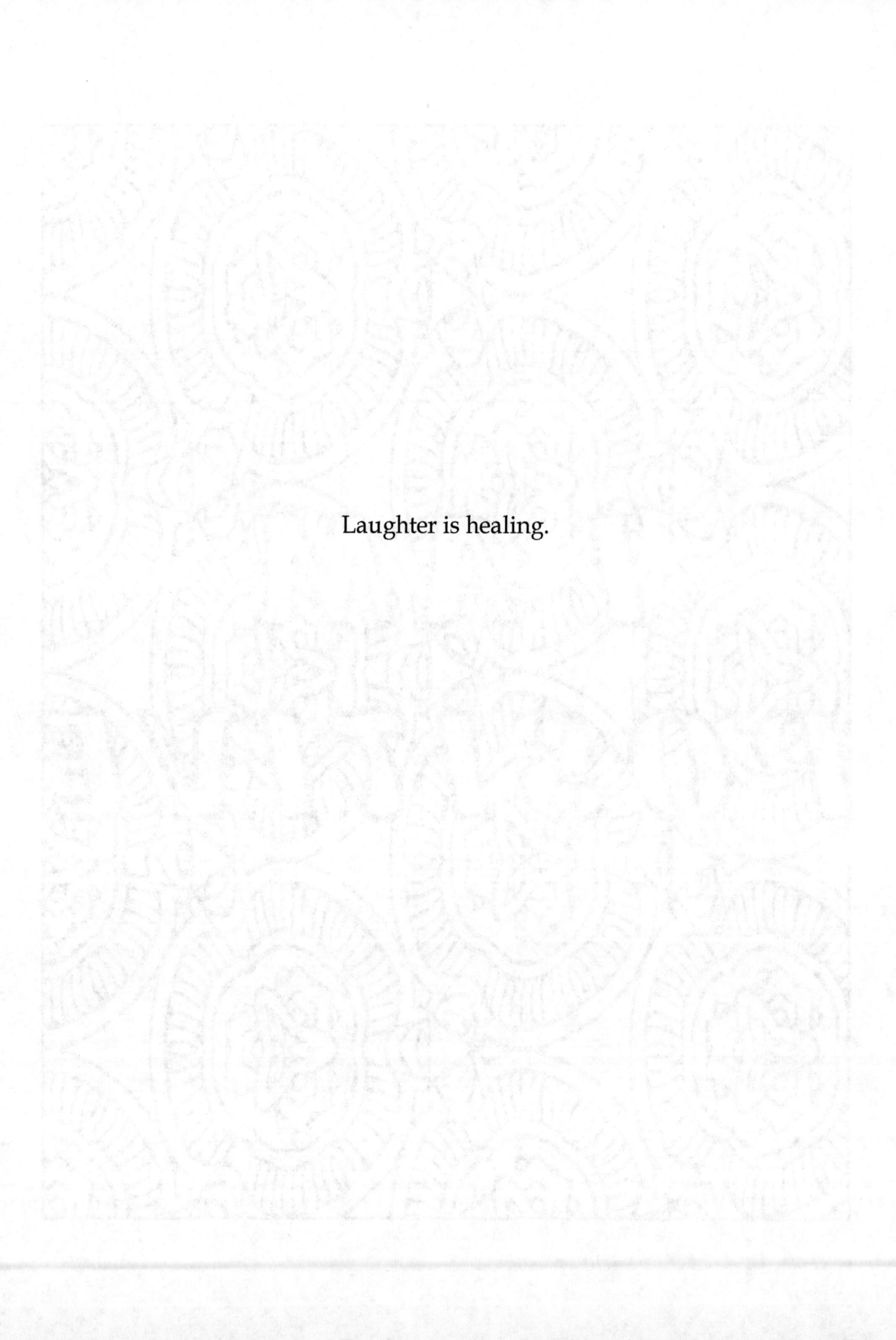

Laughter is healing.

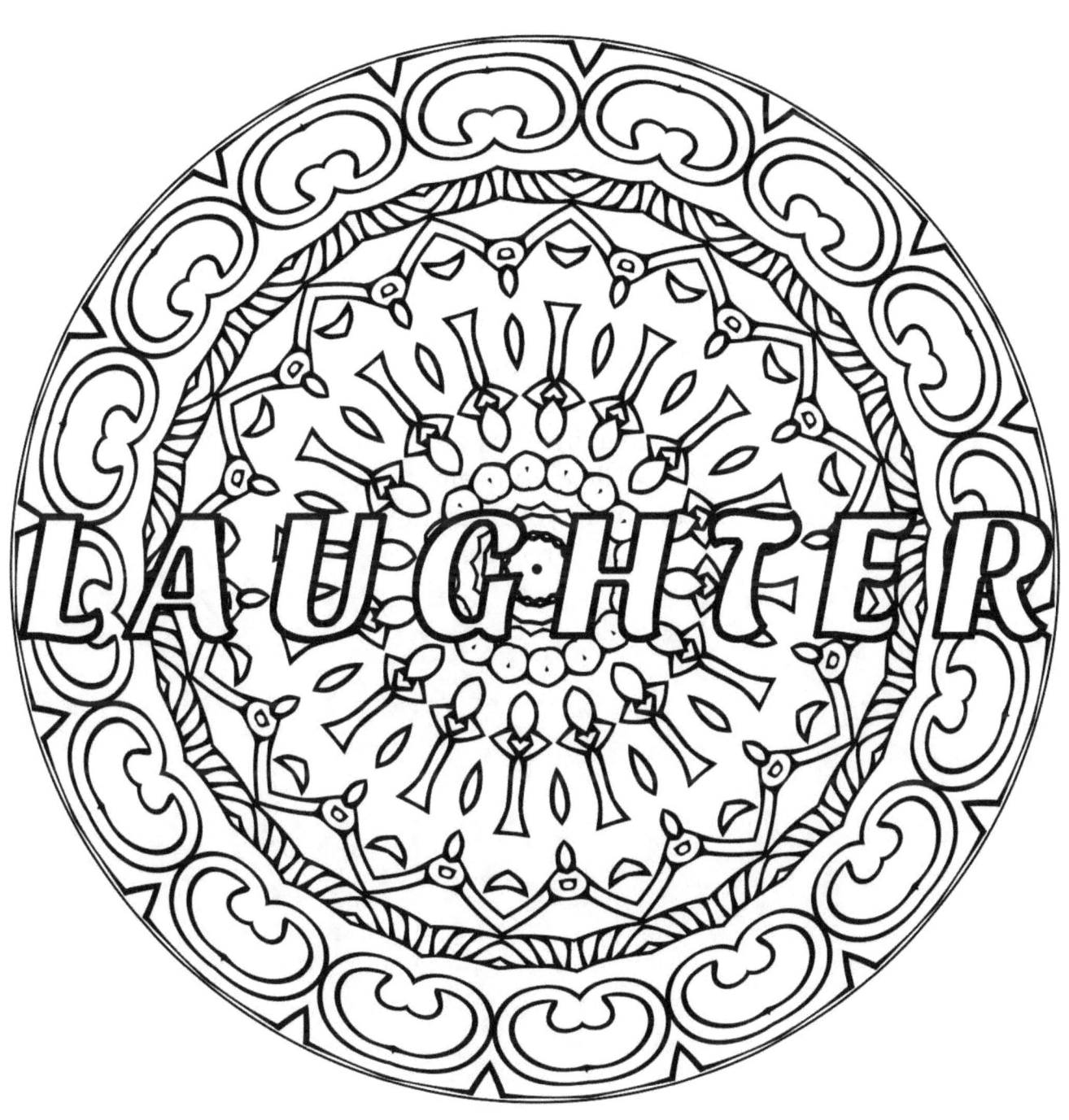

What we imagine
we create.
Imagine the best.
Allow yourself
to dream your best life
into reality.

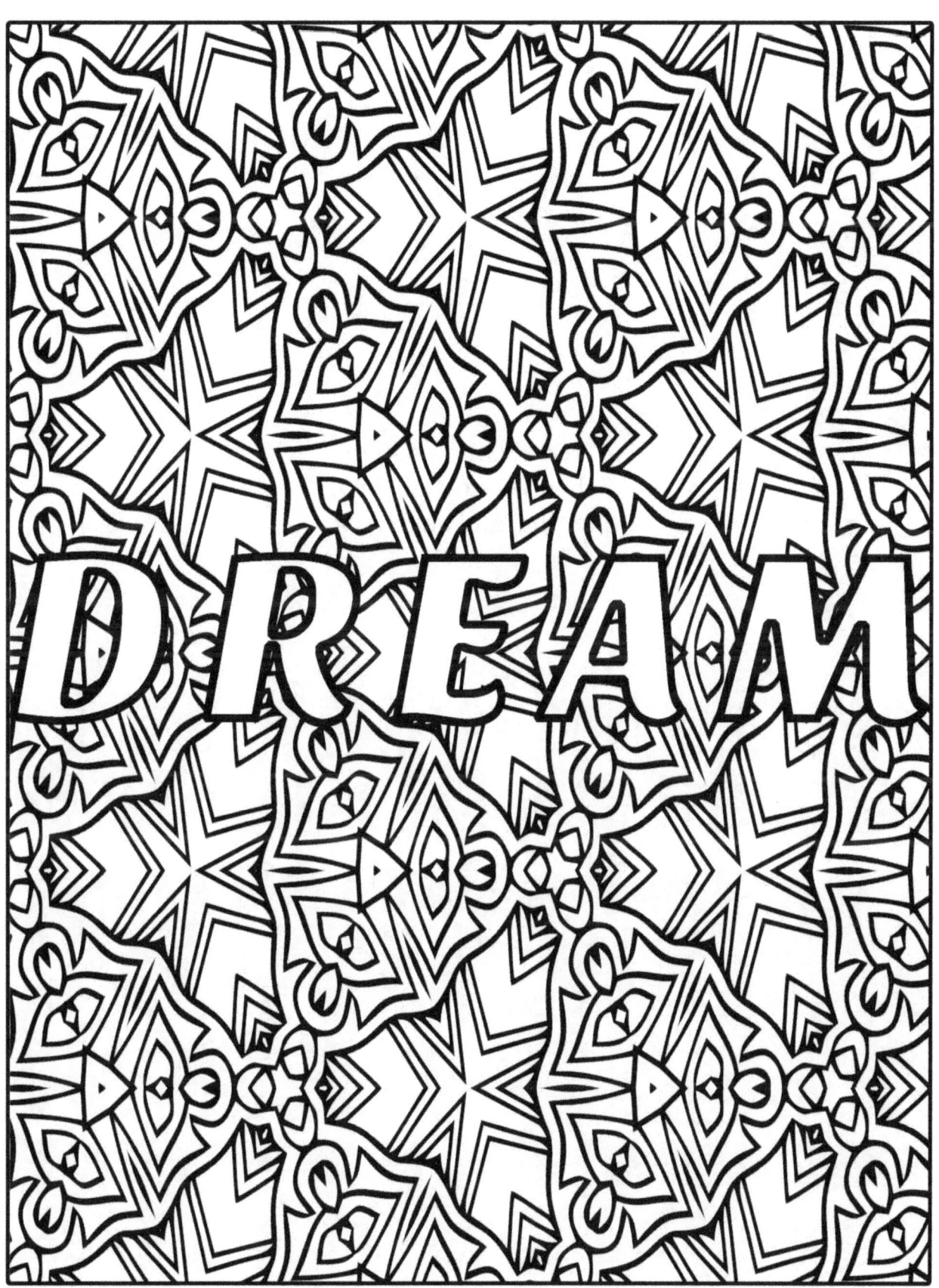

True awareness starts
when we stop labeling,
judging, and analyzing.

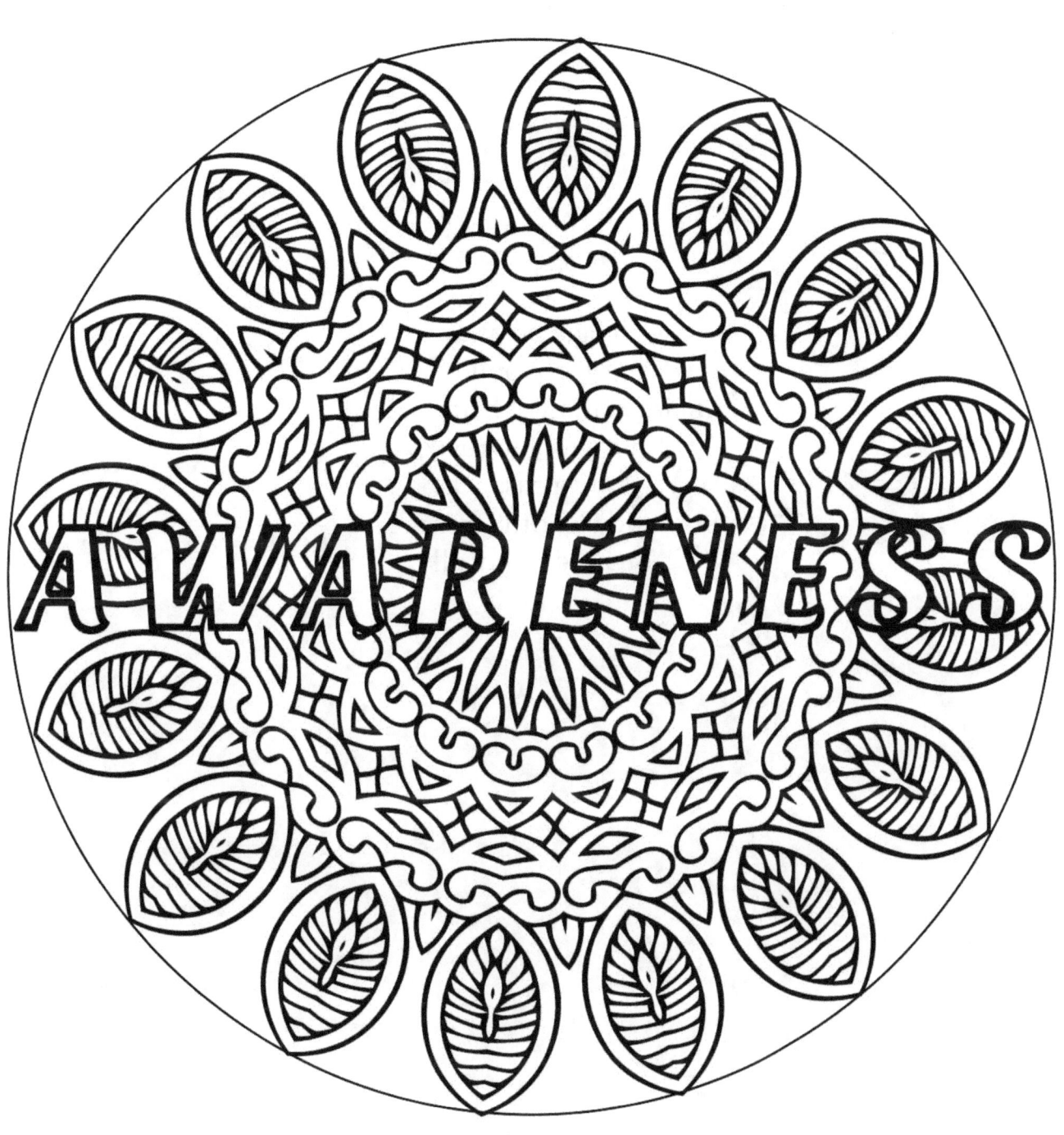

The breath
is not only
an indication of being alive,
it's a tool to relax,
release,
and clear the mind.
Breathe mindfully.

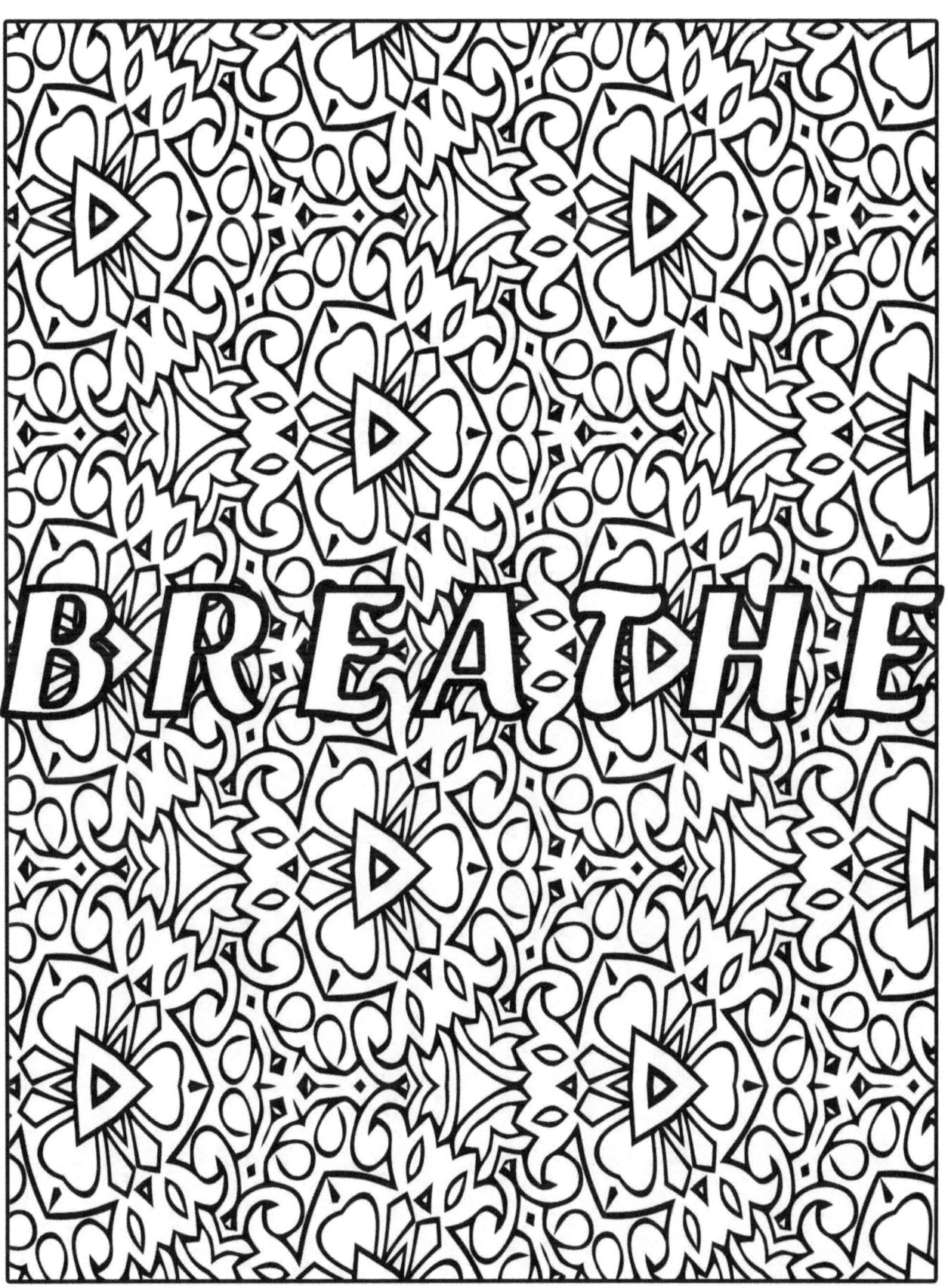

Your intuition
is there to guide you
when you know how to listen.
It whispers into your ears,
shows you visions,
speaks into your body,
and surfaces wisdom into
your thoughts.

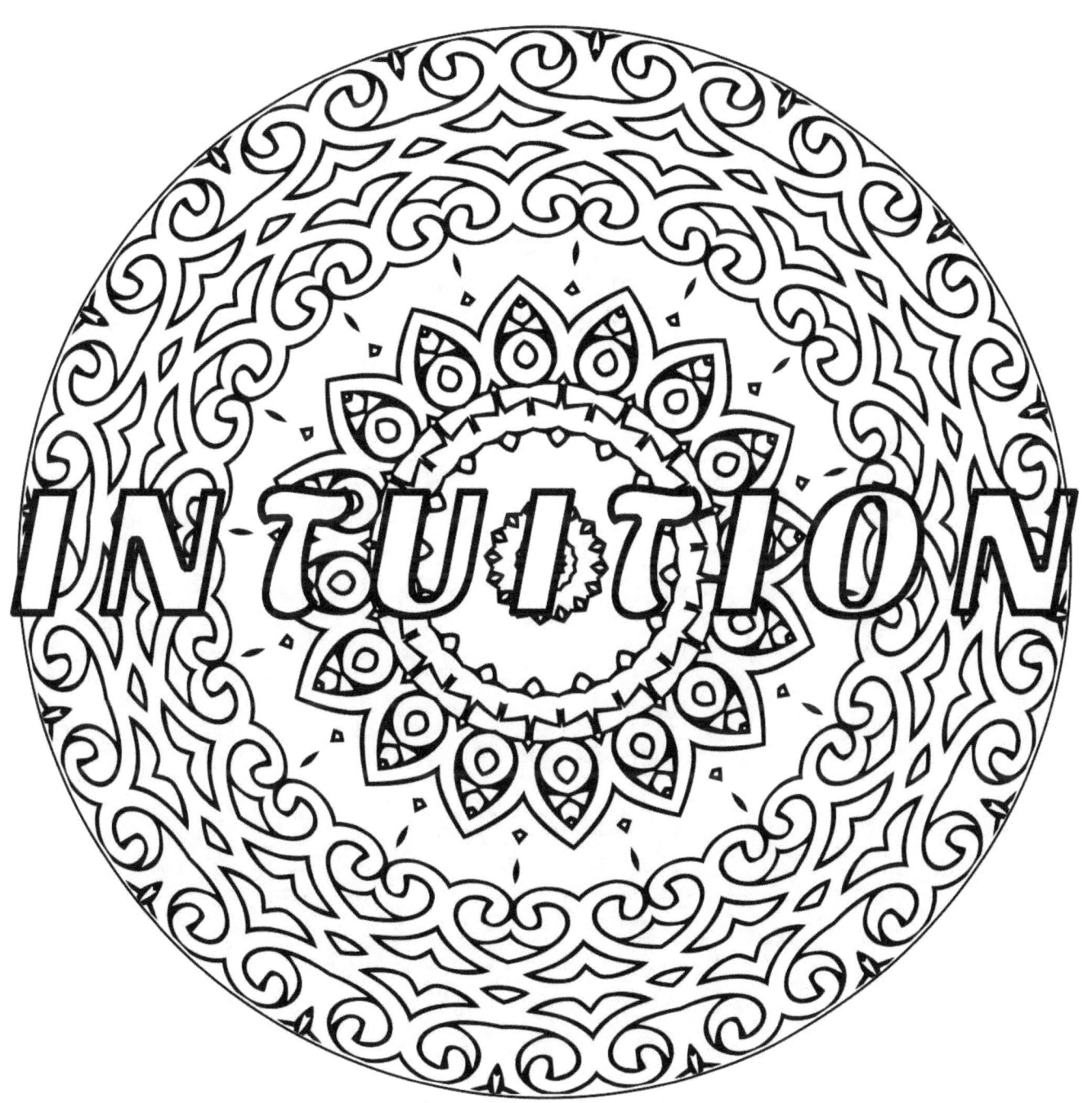

Generosity
is an outward expression
of gratitude.

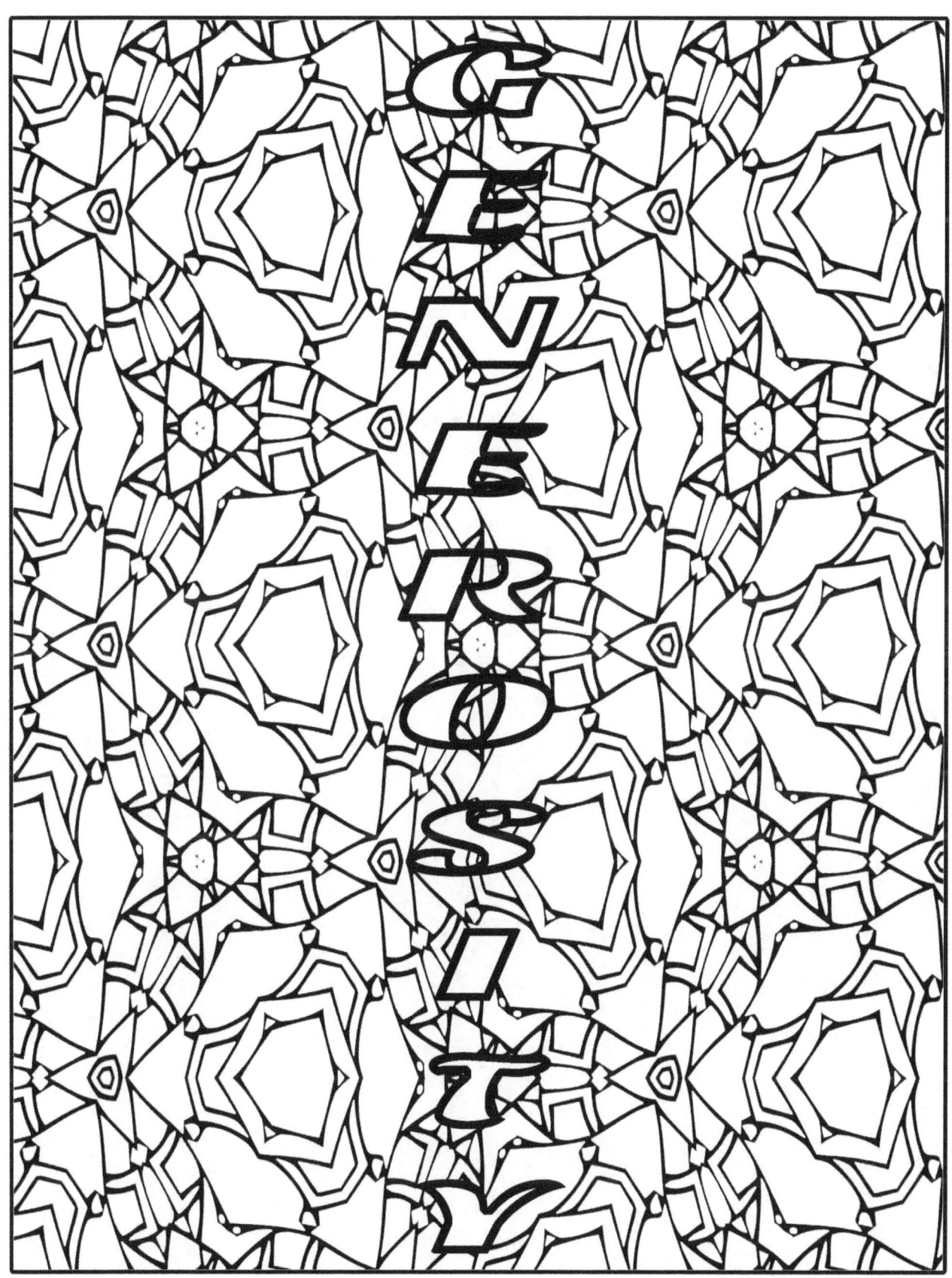

GENEROSITY

You are capable
of experiencing
the best in every
moment.
Just choose.

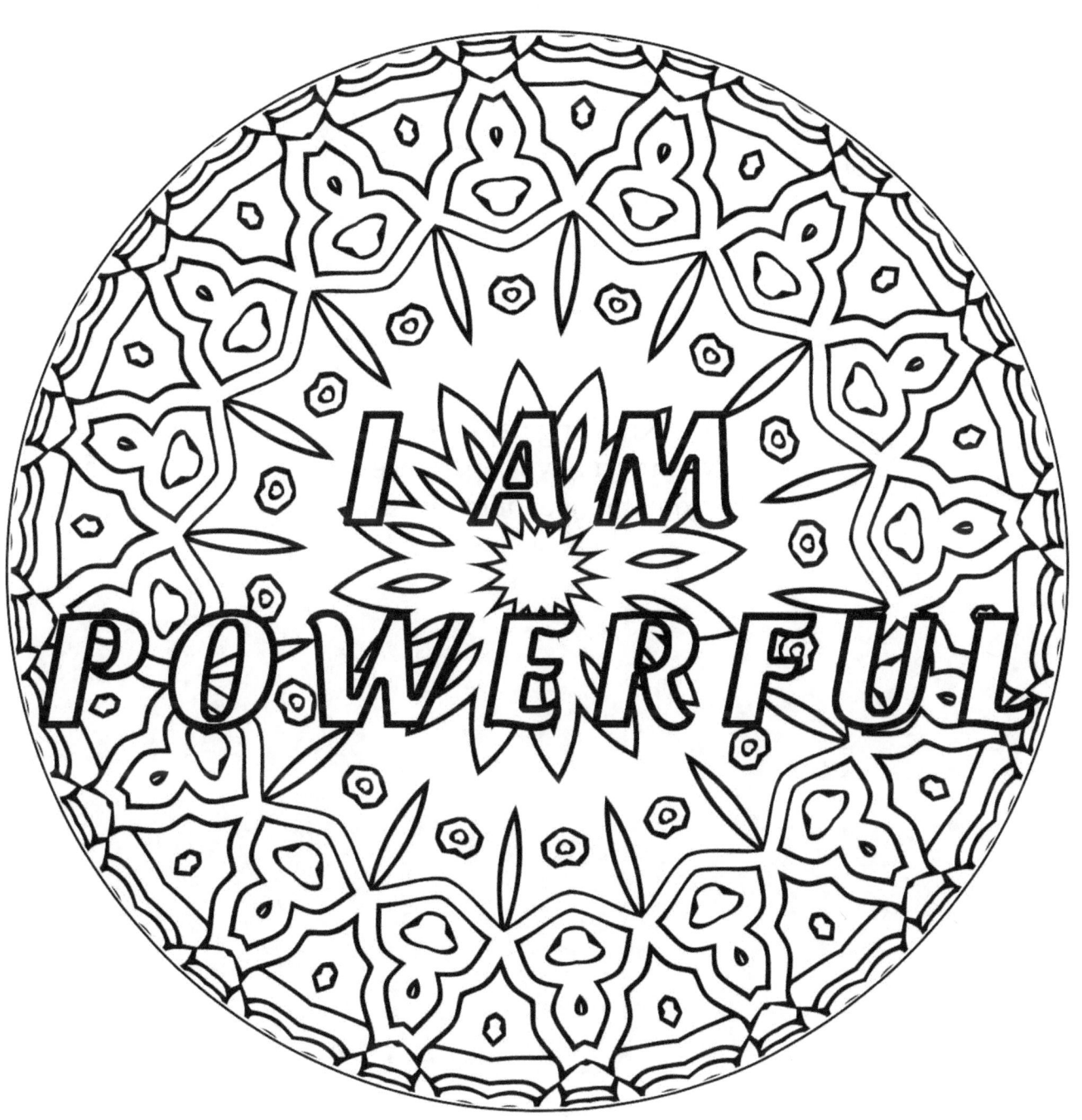

Knowing happens
when you have experienced
something enough times
to believe it.

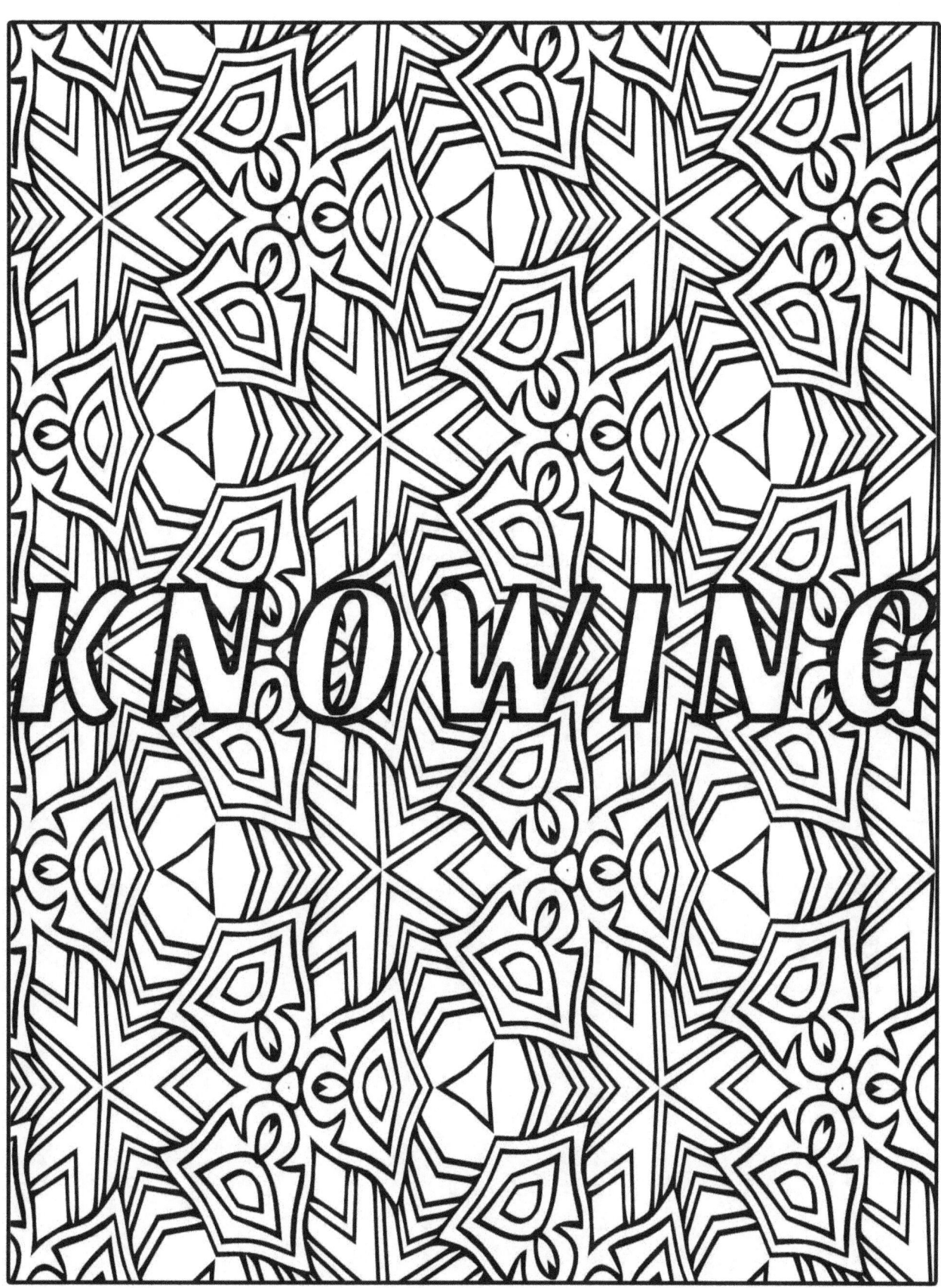

Vitality
is a vibration
of true health
and well-being.
It's in you.

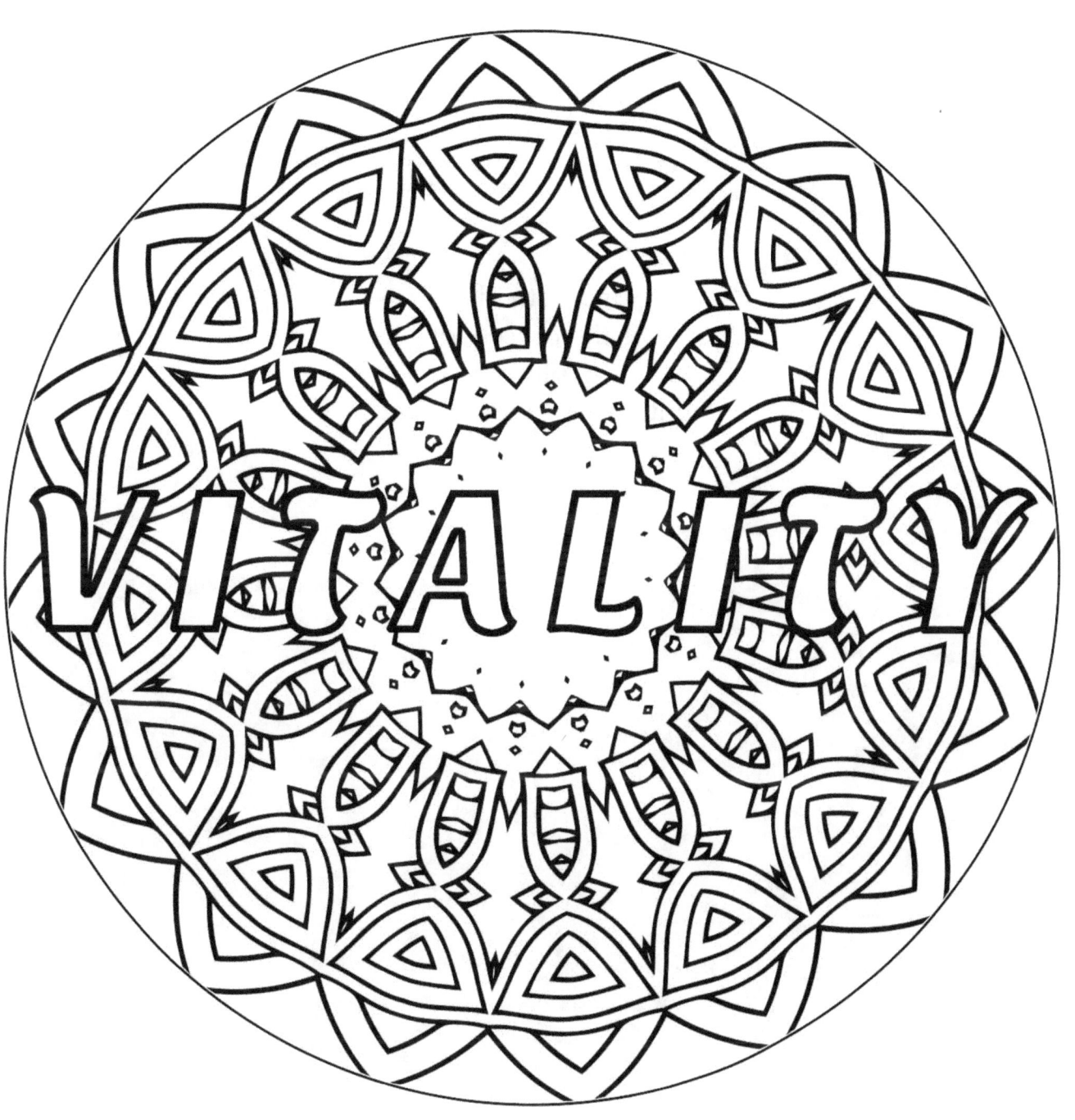

Understanding
is the process of
exploring
until things make sense.

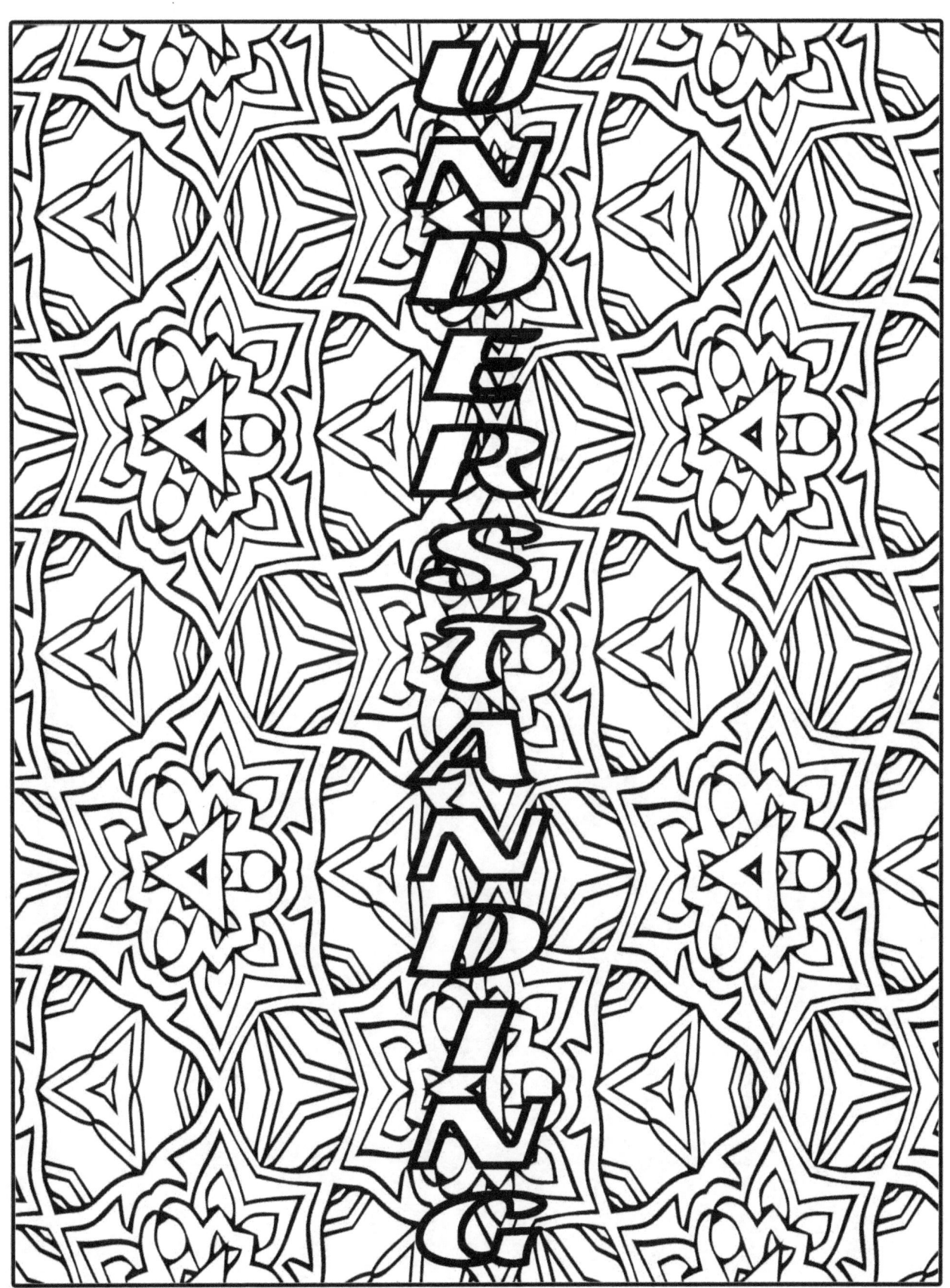

All matter is energy.
All energy recycles into different forms.
Nothing ever is gone.

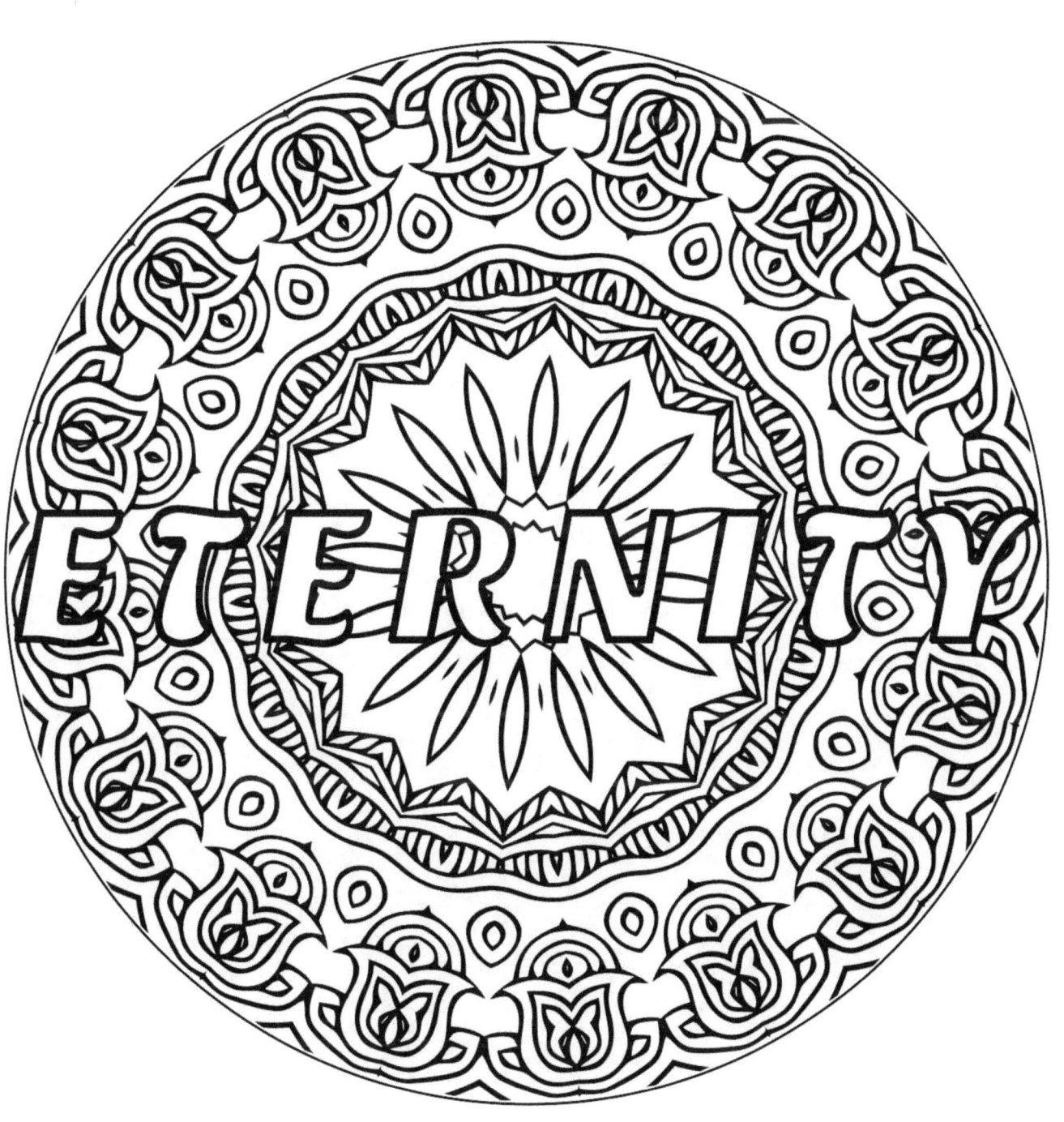

All of the information
in the Universe
is available
to those who are
conscious enough
to access it.
To know more,
think less.
Open to the information
and let it come to you.

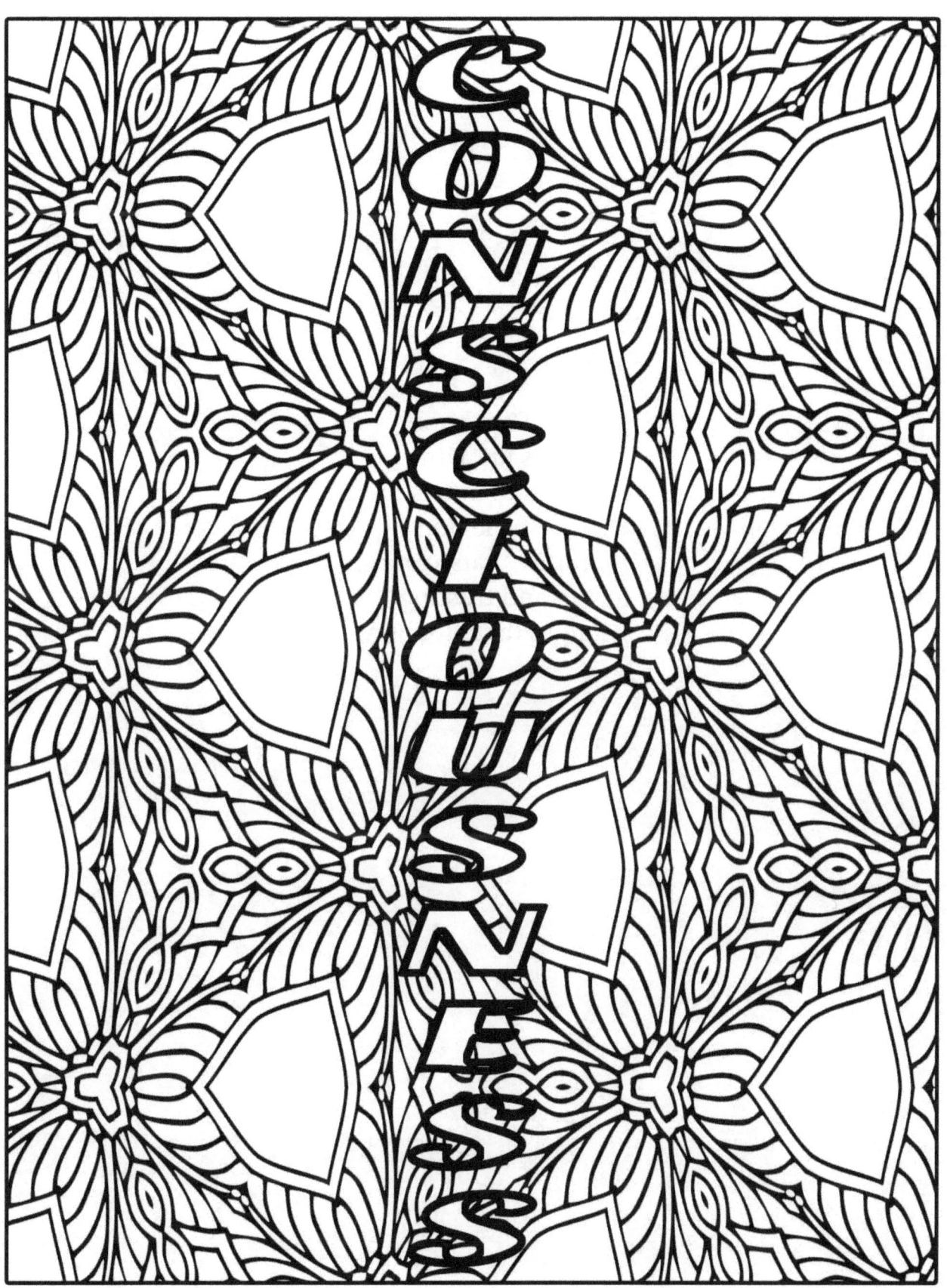

True hope
is knowing
rather than wishing,
believing
rather than fearing,
and trusting
rather than doubting.

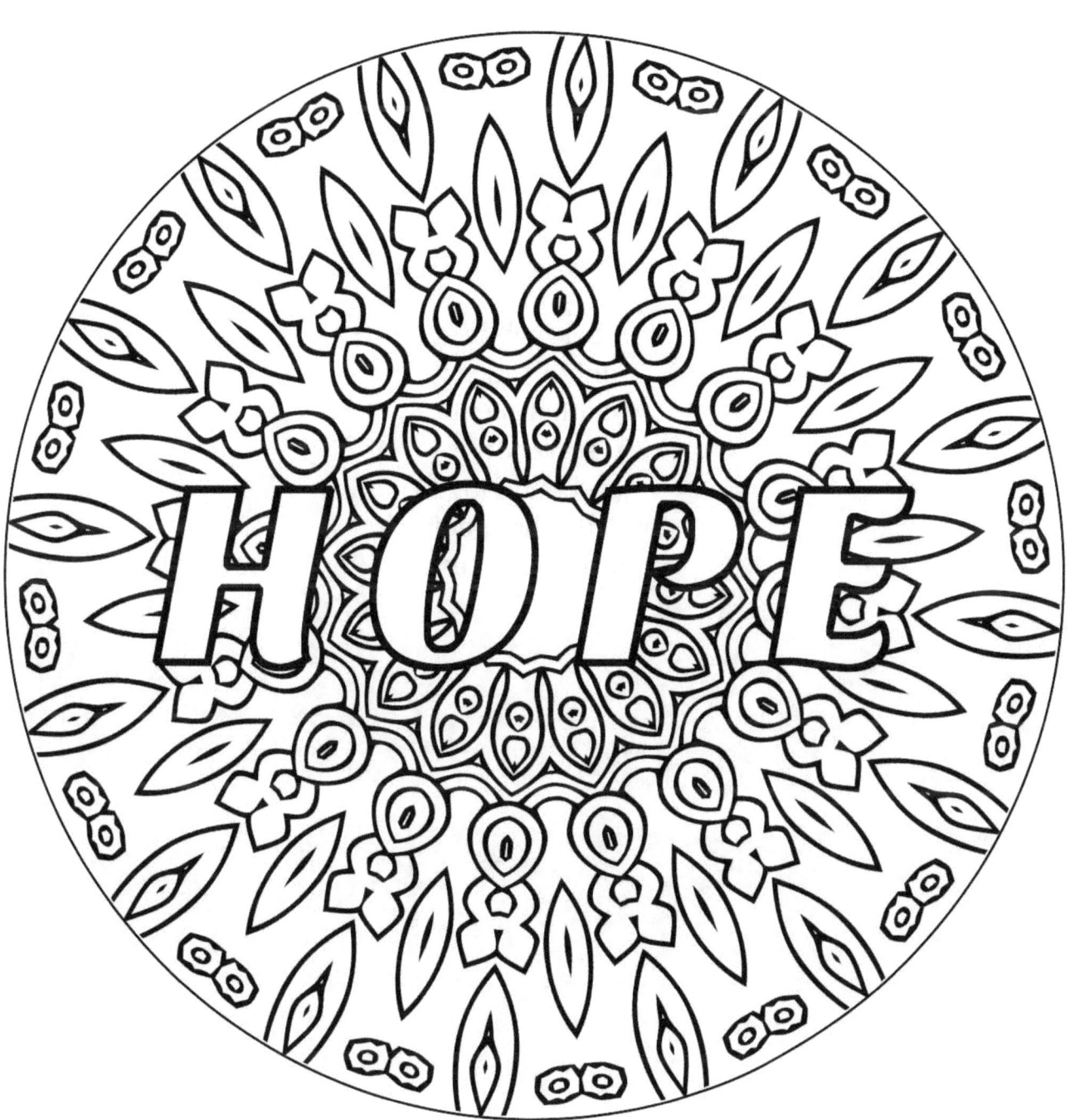

Serenity is
inner peace
contentment
surrender
and knowing
that all is happening
for the very best.

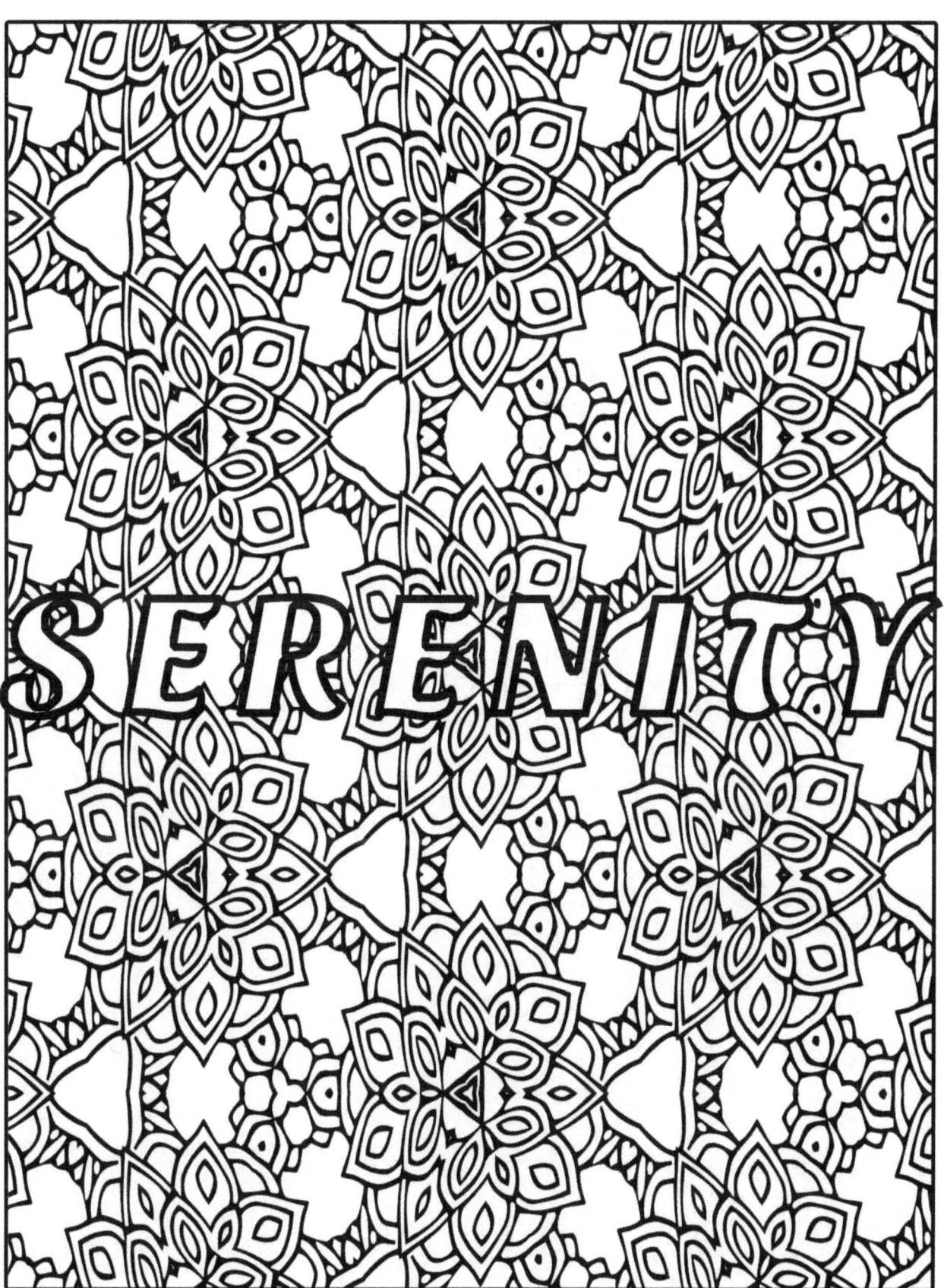

Reiki means Life Force Energy.
It is an energy healing method
for pain relief, stress relief,
and better health.
The beautiful thing about it
is that it also makes one
acutely aware
of being connected
to something bigger
than one's individual
experience of existence.

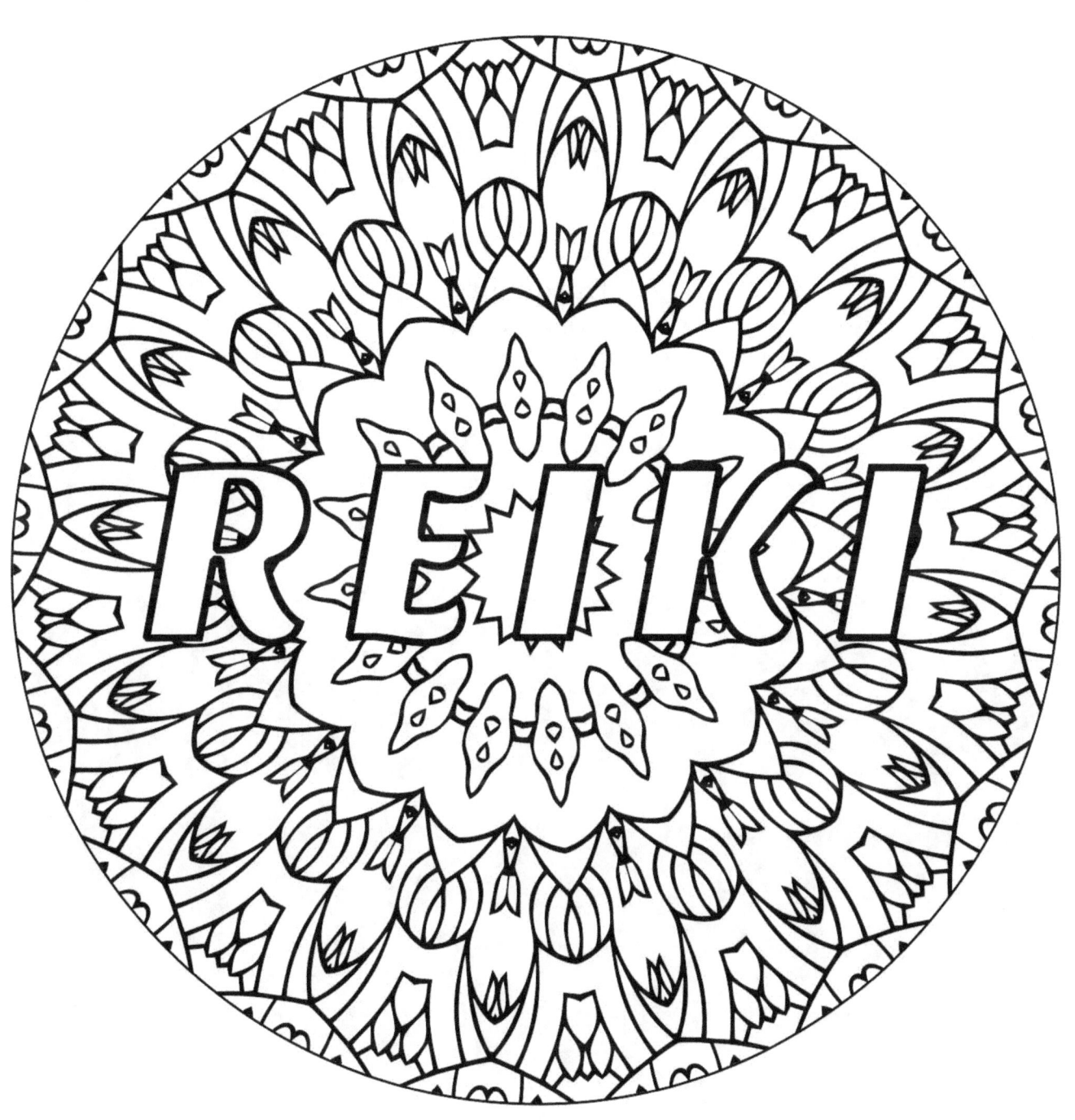

Tranquility
is a deep sense
of peace.

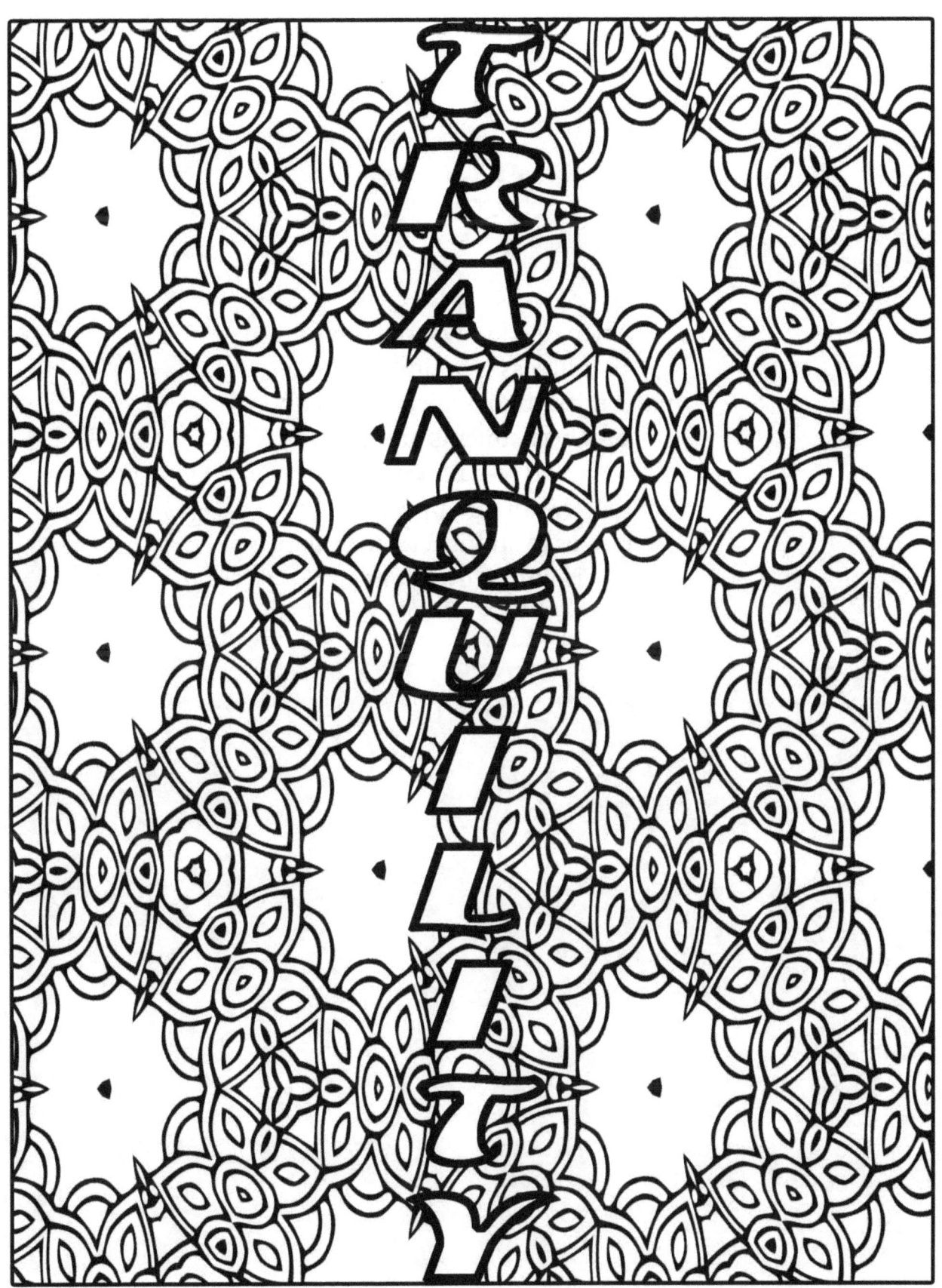

When one knows for certain
that illness is an imbalance
in the mind-body-spirit connection,
and adjustments are made
to re-balance,
healing happens.
The power to shift back into balance
is within everyone.

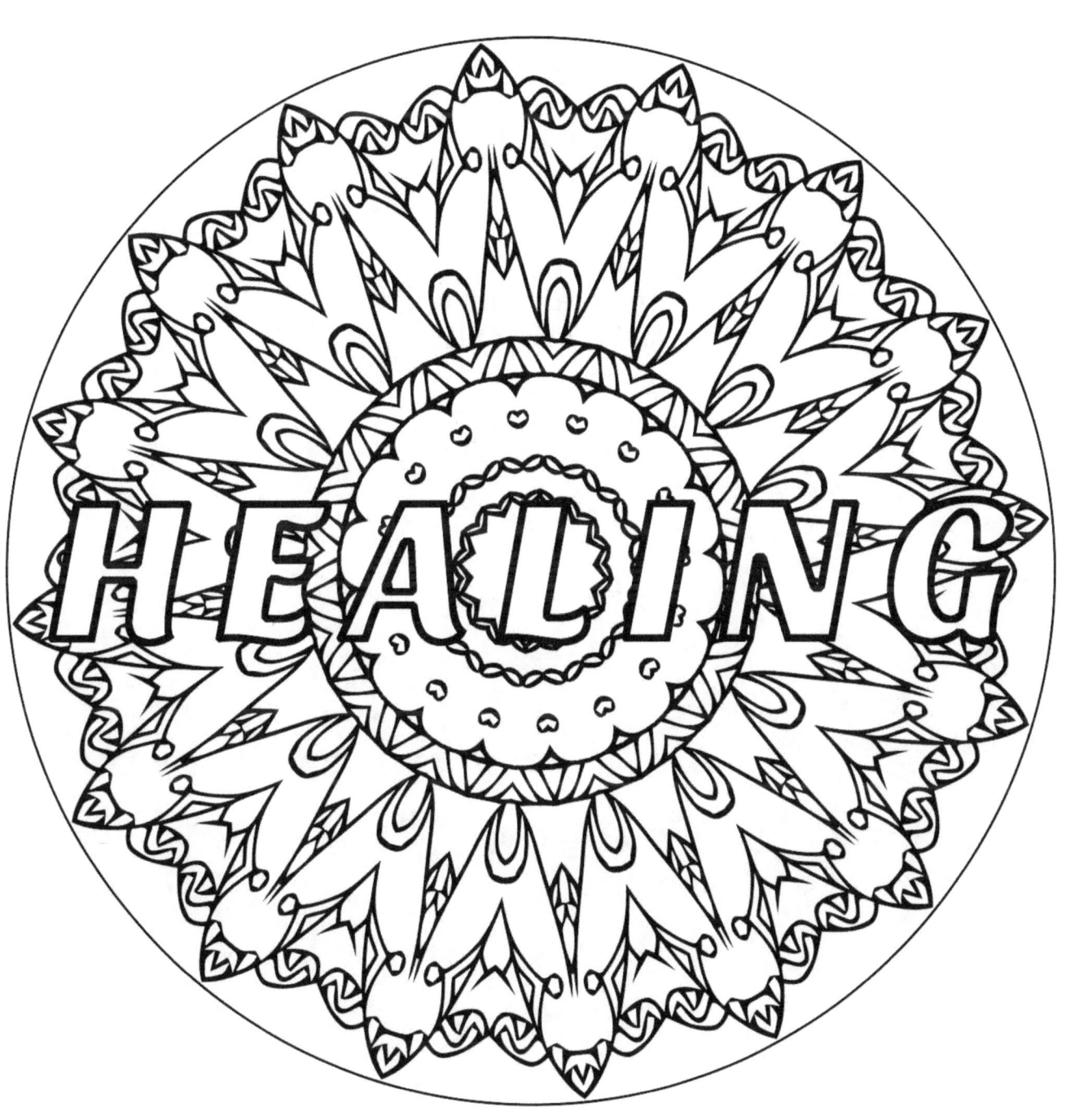

Angels are with you,
waiting to be called on
happy to help you,
and loving you
without condition.

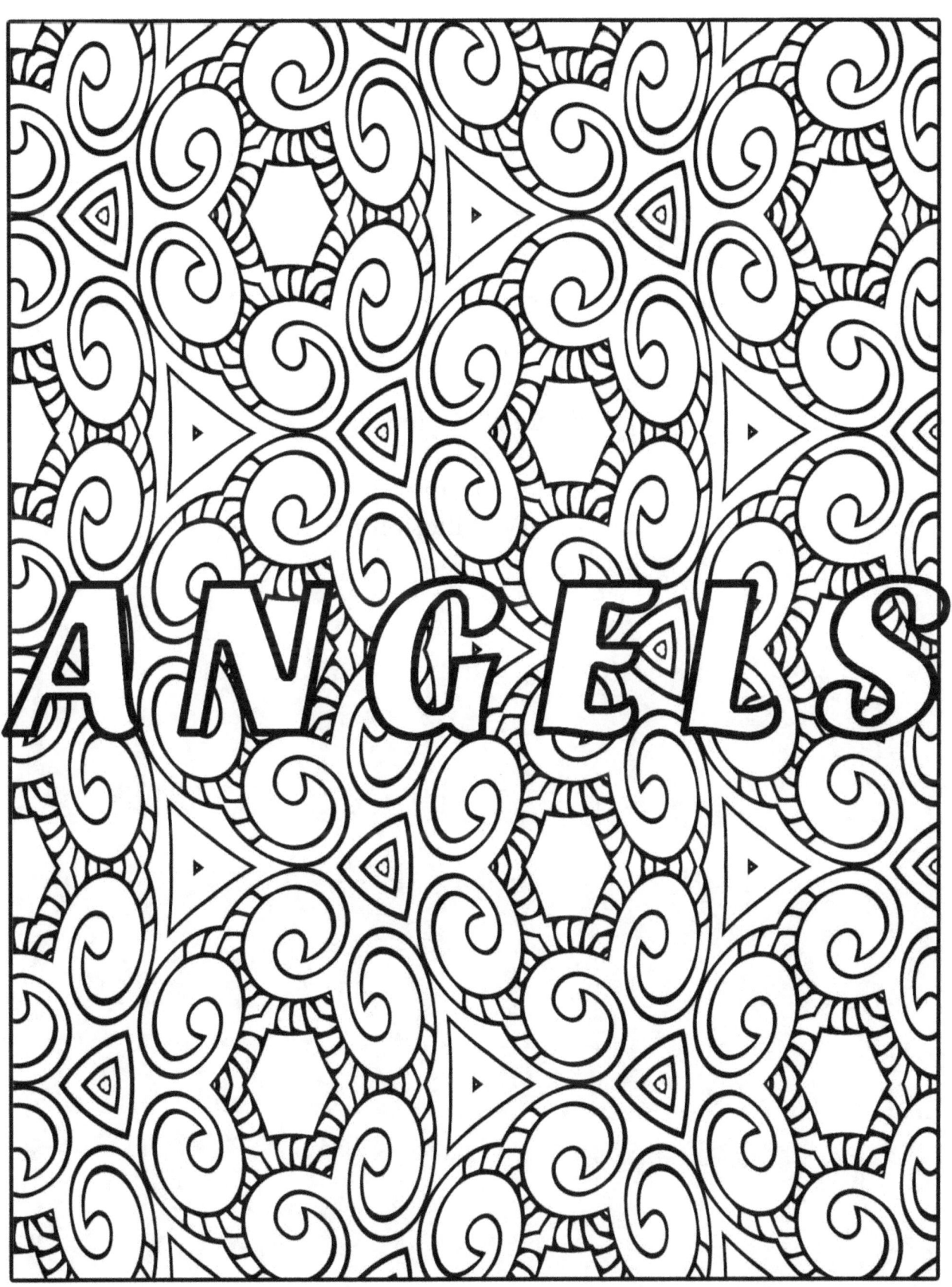

We are all complete,
whole,
and worthy.
All else is illusion.

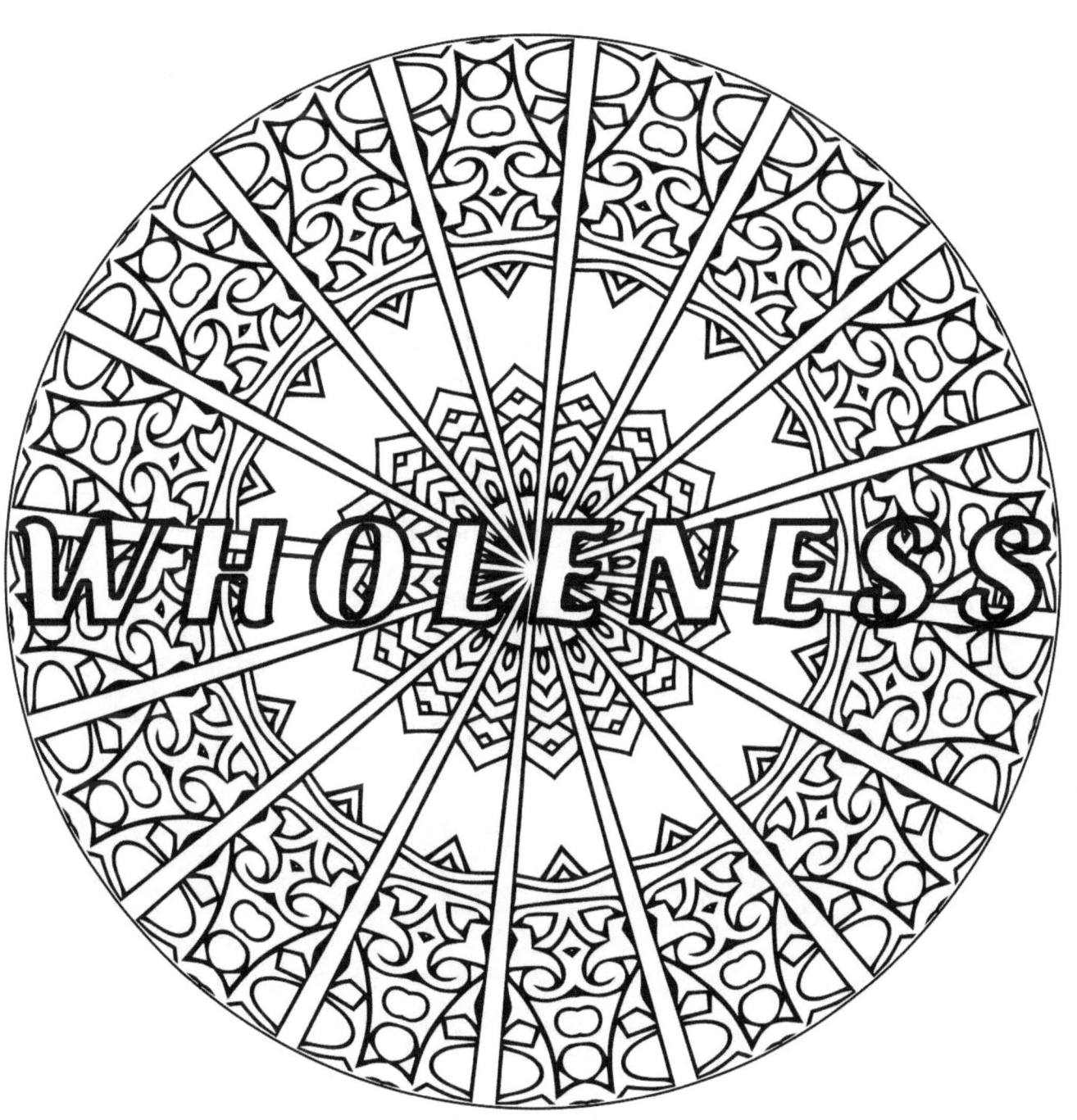

To be content,
accept.
Accept that you are in the right place
at the right time,
and that you can change
what does not serve you,
reject what isn't about you,
and invite in your highest and best
any time you choose to.

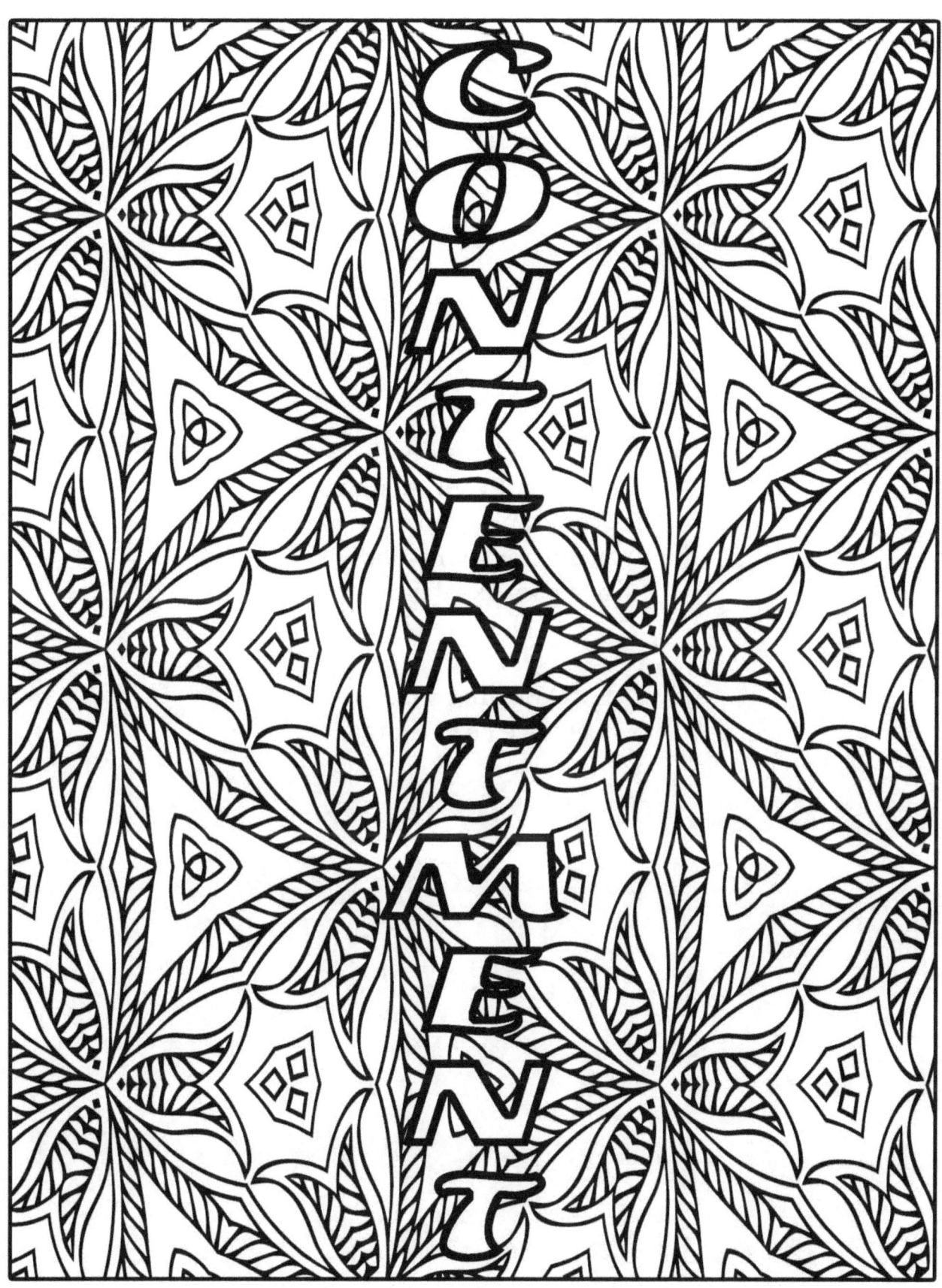

Look inside.
You are not your thoughts.
They come and go like the river.
You are not your emotions.
They pass like the clouds.
What's left?
Love.
You are Love.
Let Love be in charge.

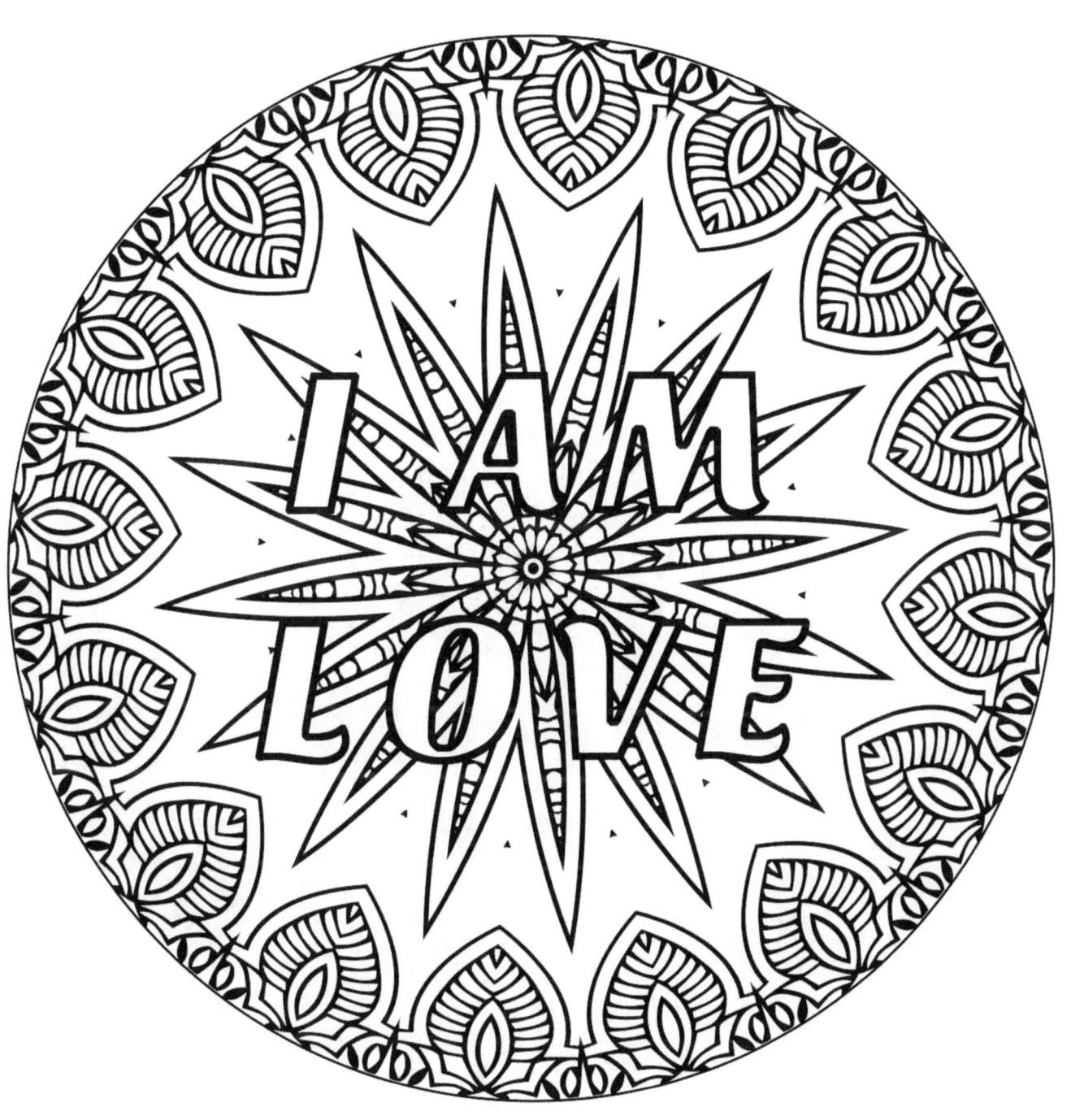

Quiet your mind.
Ask your question.
Wait.
The answer will come.

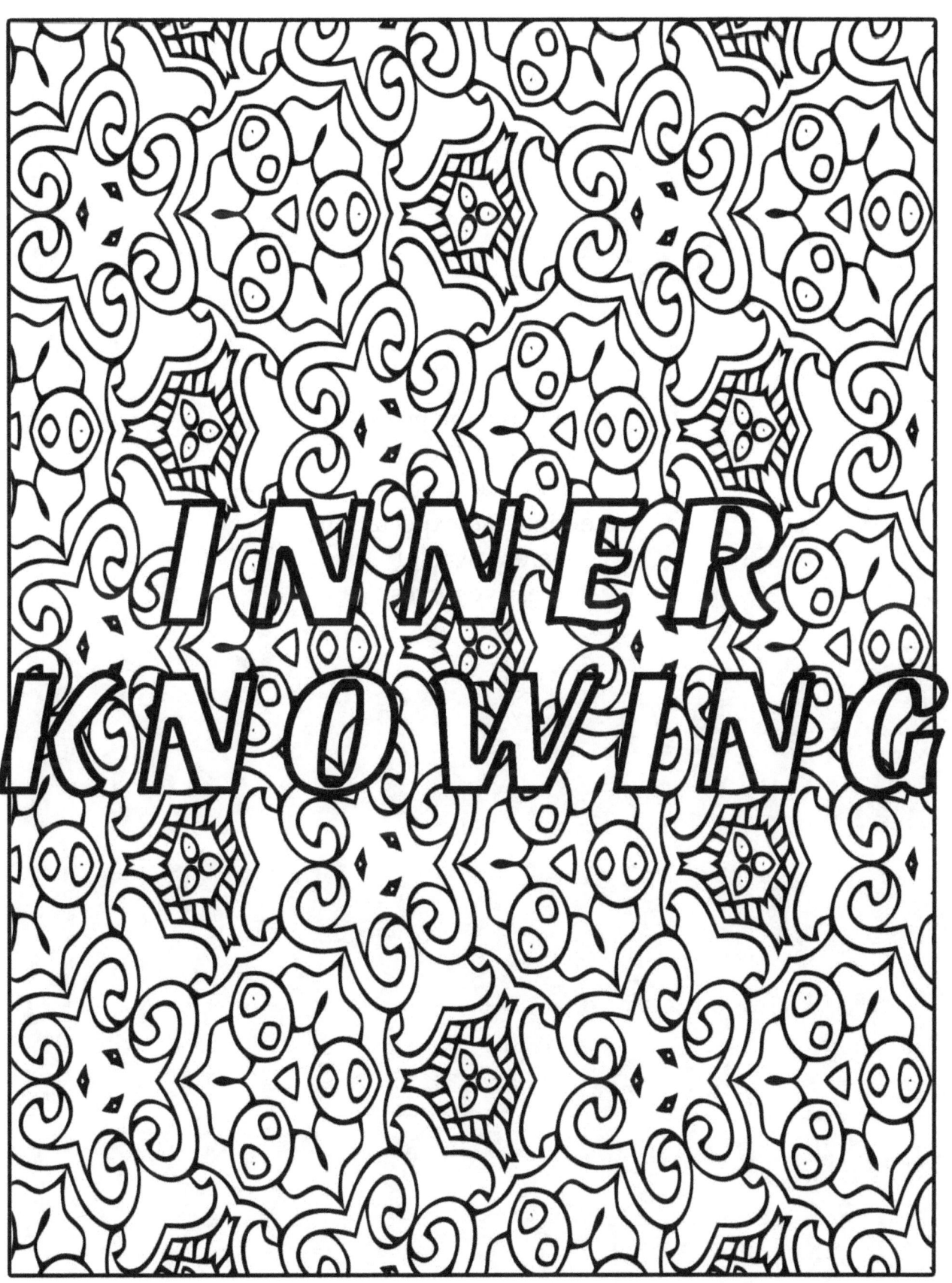

You have the power
to attract the best
into your life.
Intention and expectation
are powerful
creative forces.

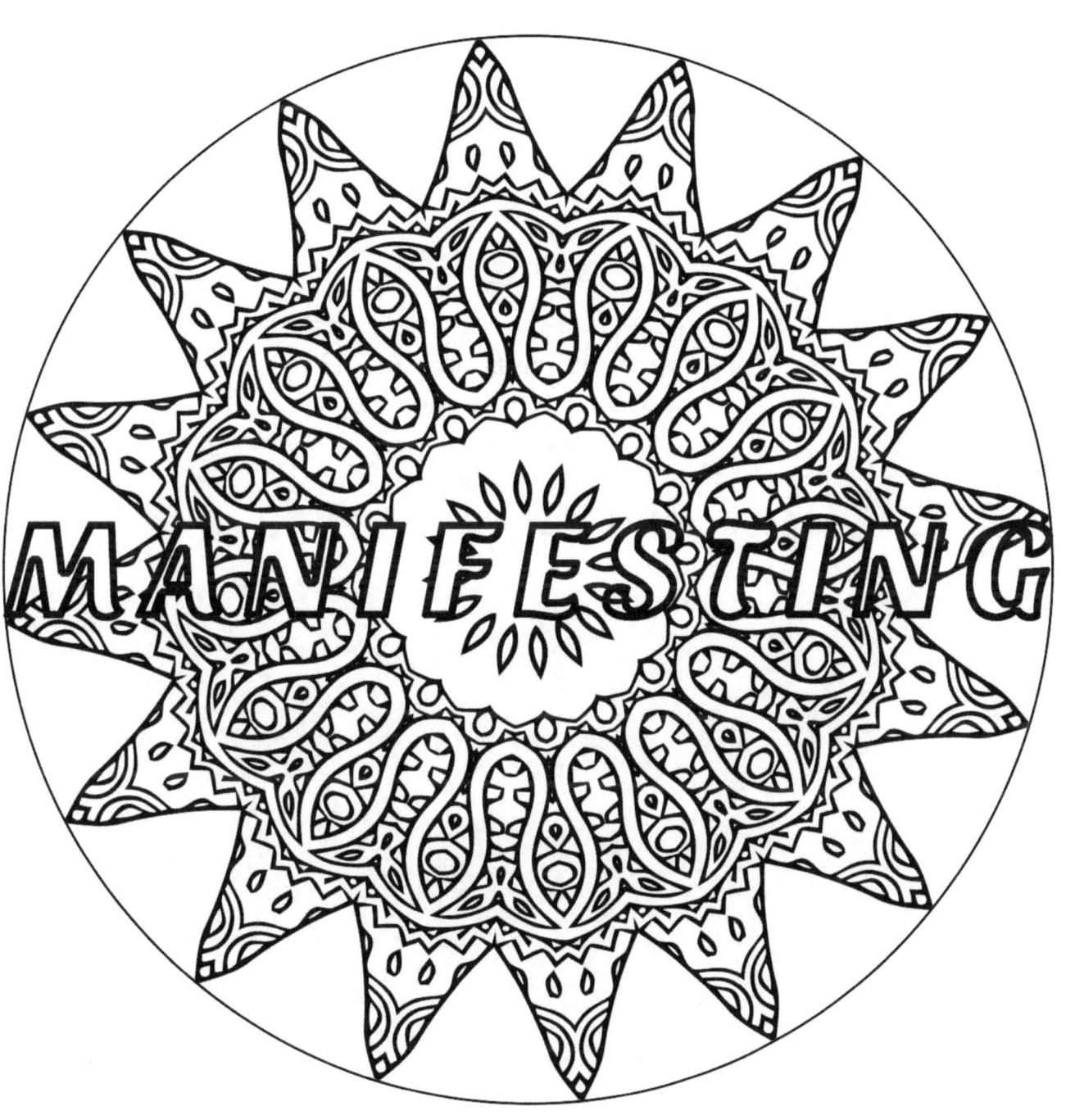

What are you passionate about?
The answer to this question
is a clue
to knowing
your life's purpose.

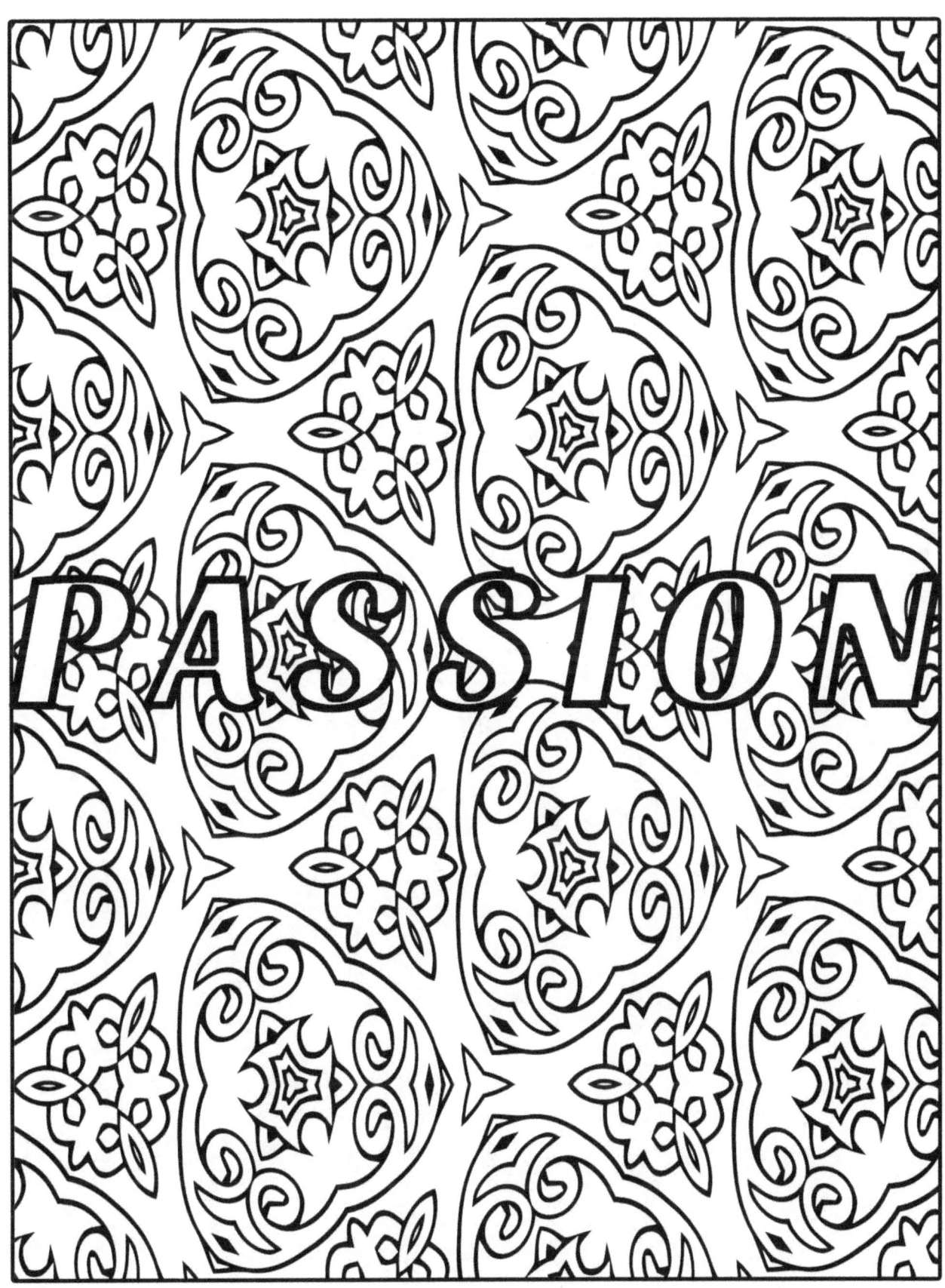

Joy
is love
expressing itself.

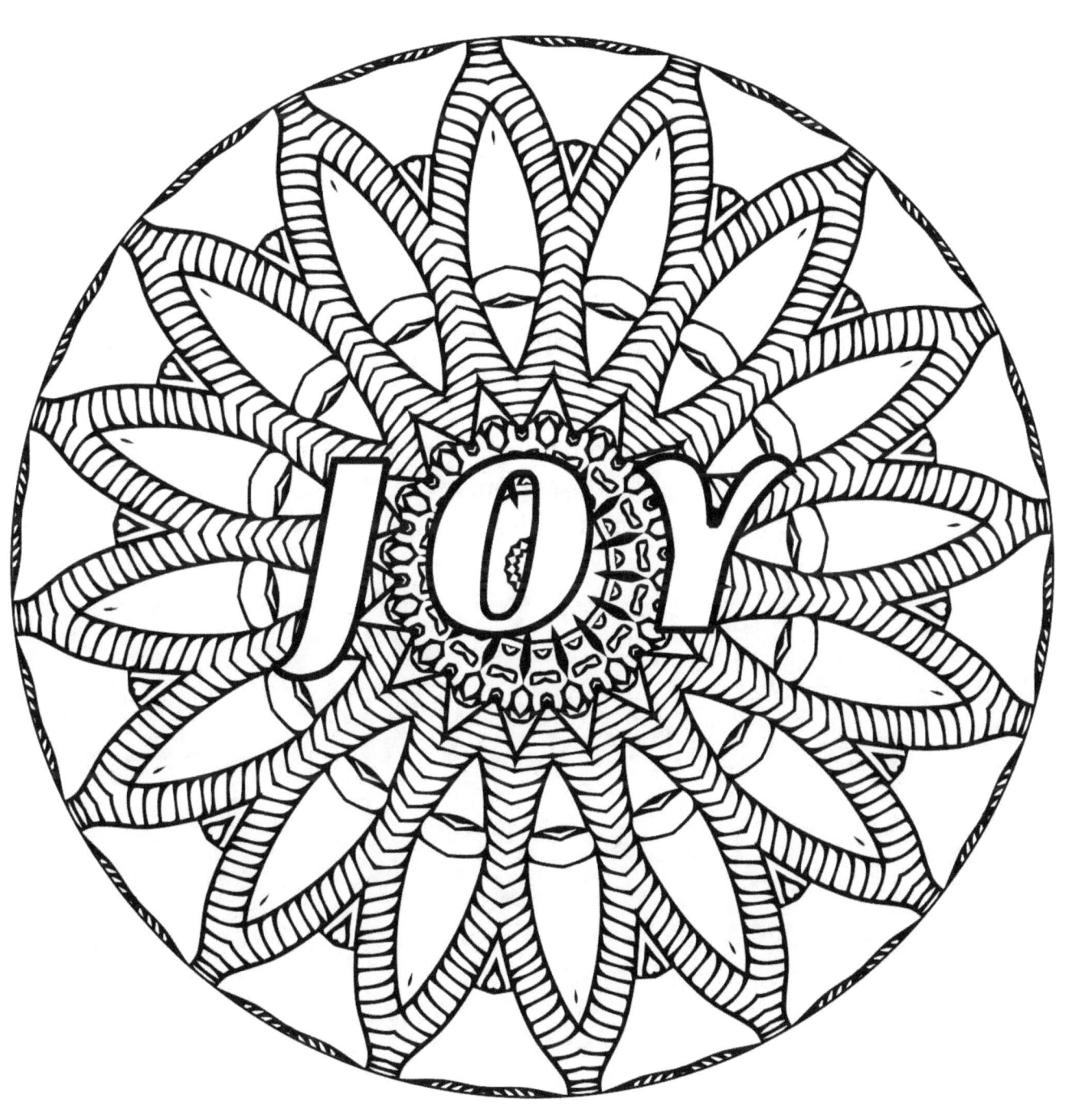

Guidance is there for you.
It speaks
in symbols,
dreams,
coincidences
goosebumps,
and whispers.

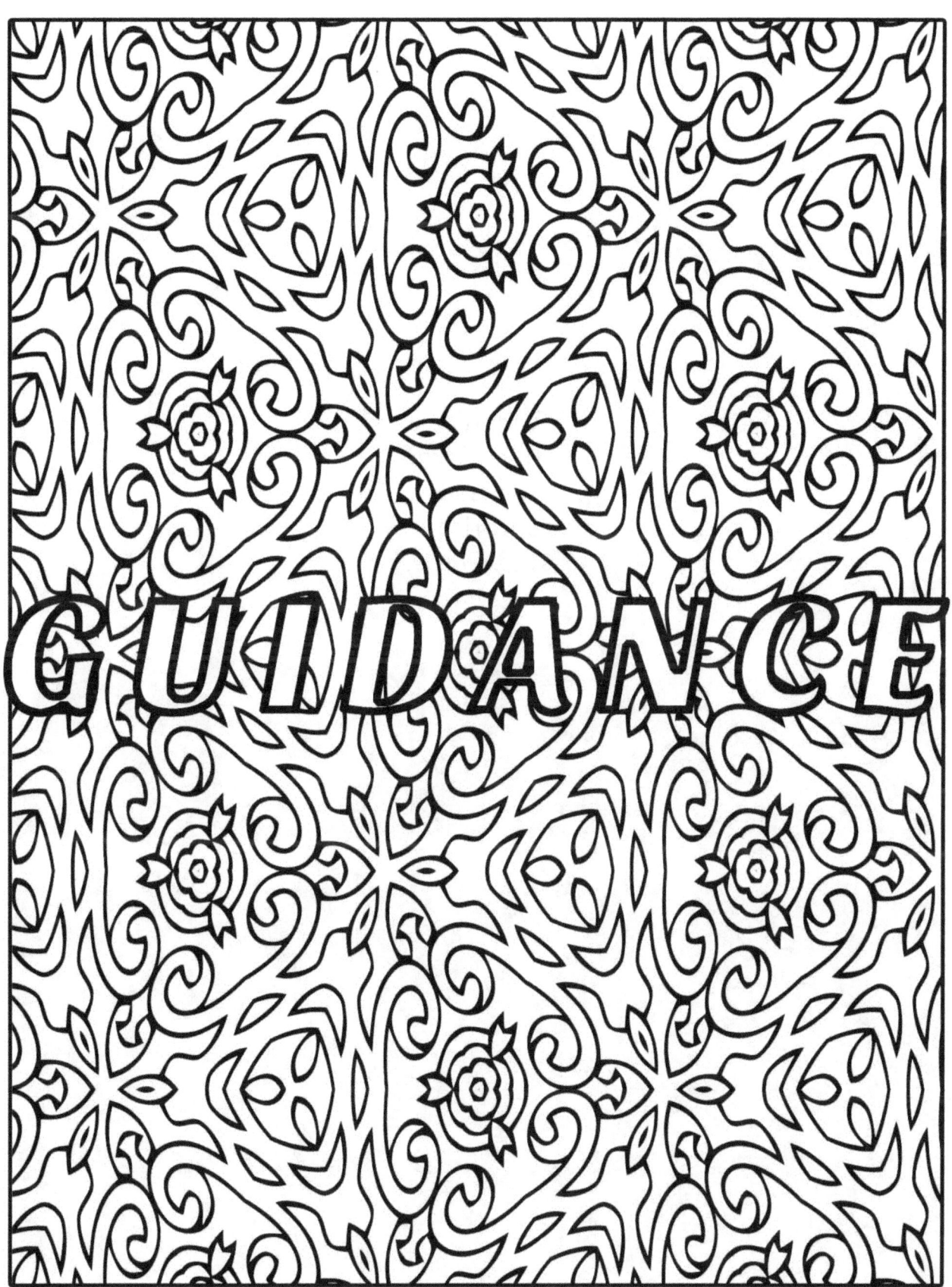

Abundance
can be found
in smiles,
surprises,
kind words,

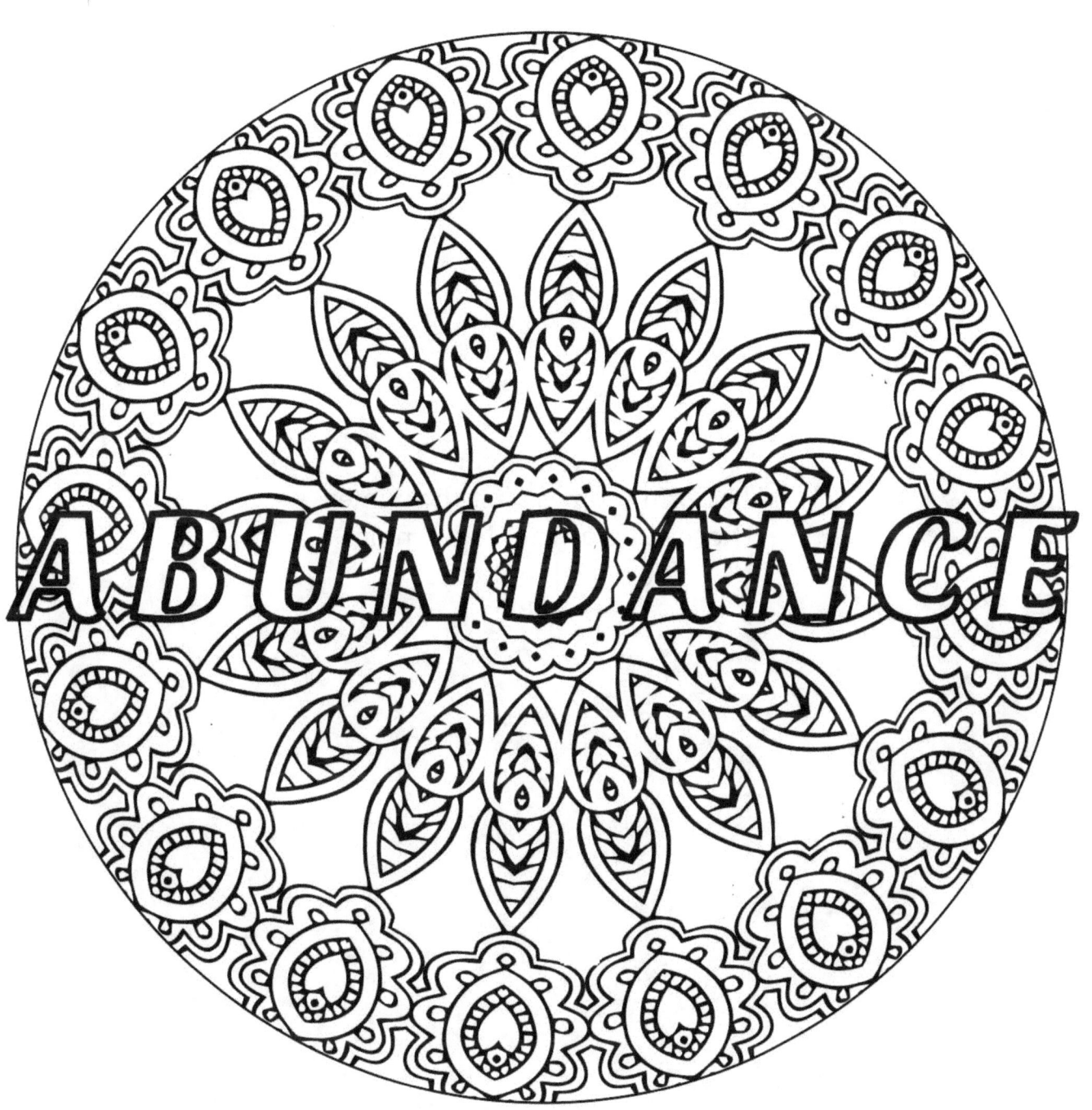

Cells regenerate.
The Spring comes after the winter.
Renewal is always happening.
Renewal is always
possible.

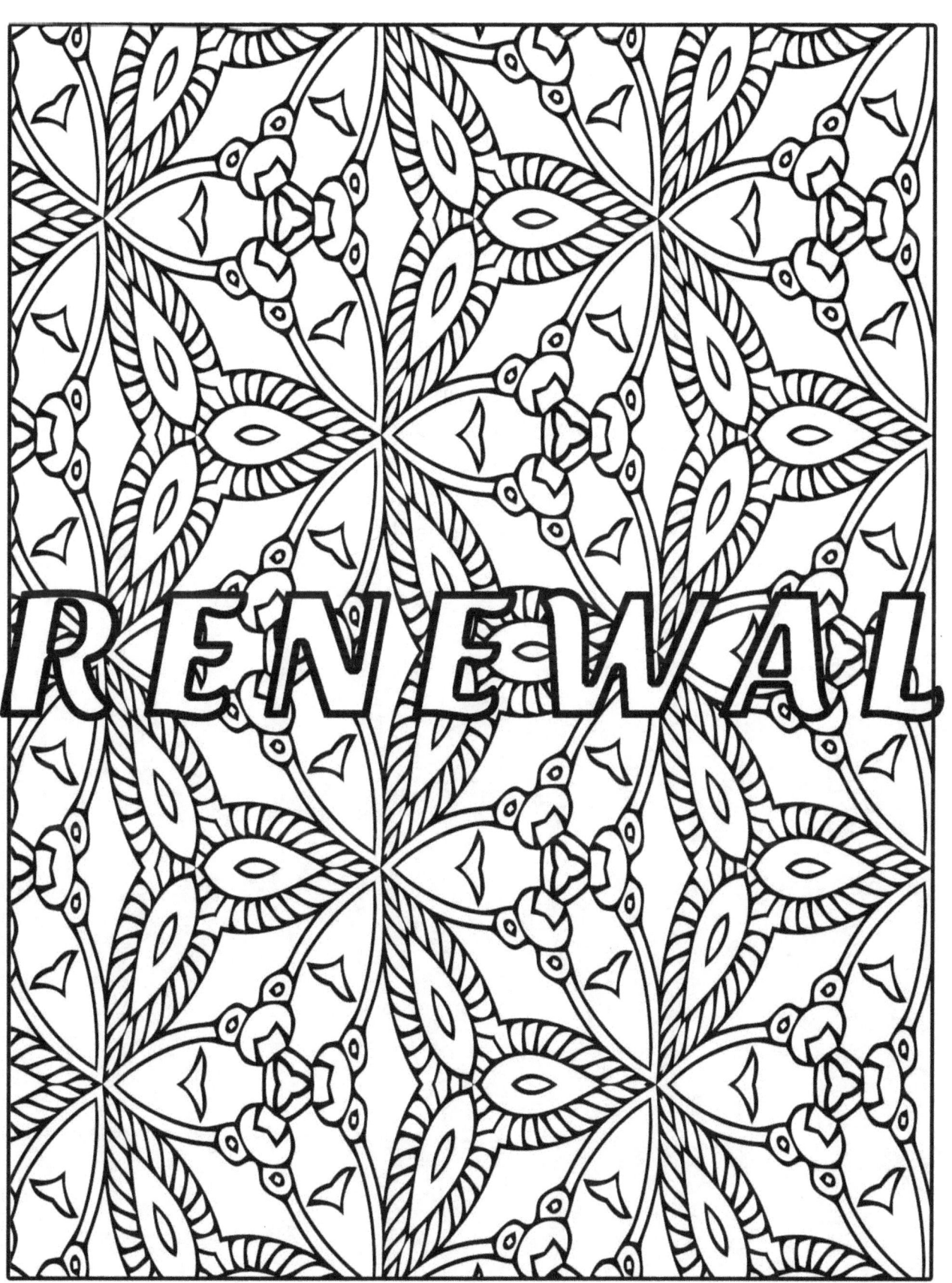

Everyone,
without exception,
is worthy of
an infinite measure
of unconditional love.

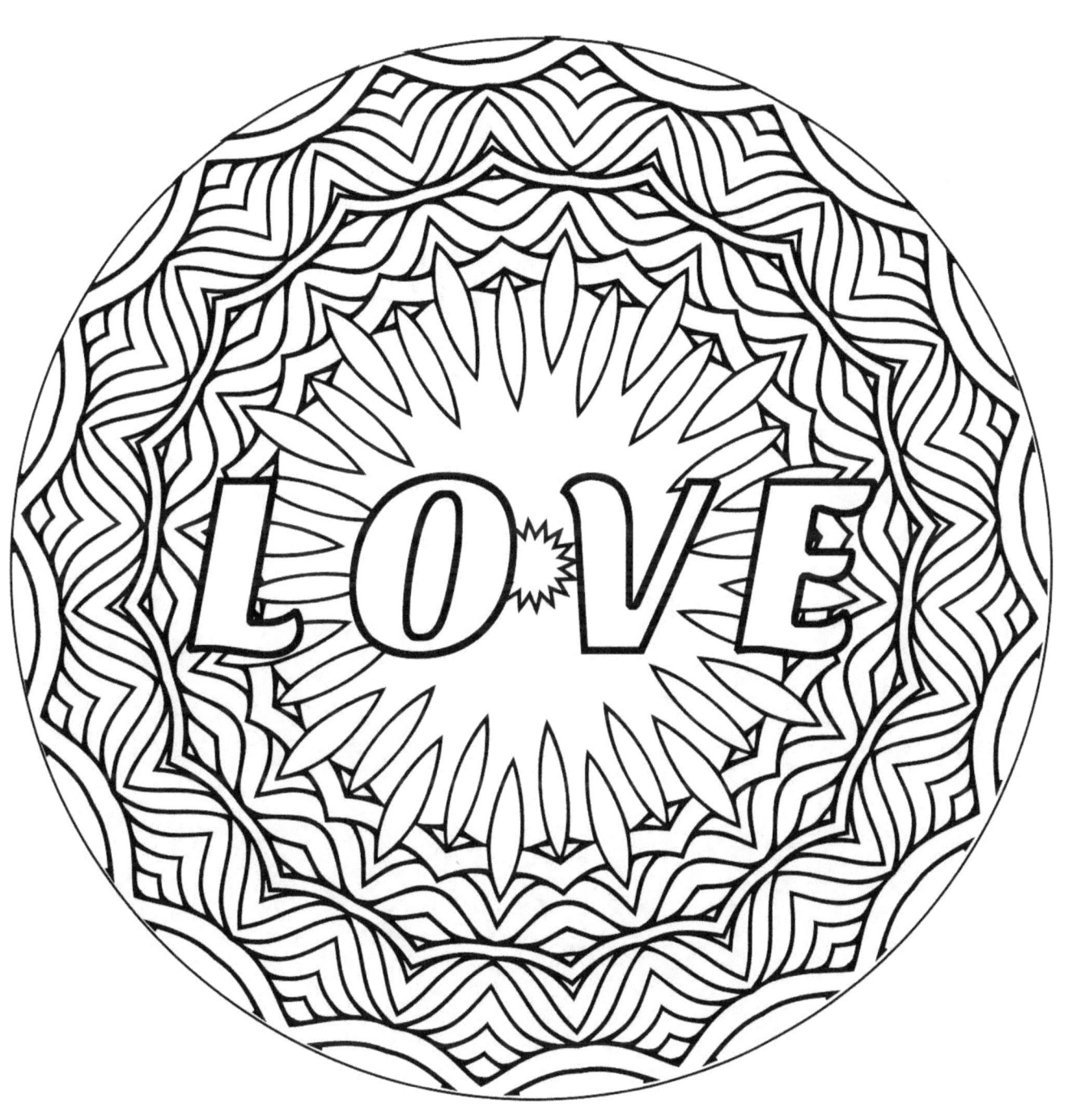

Affirm your strength.
Once cannot be confident
and stressed, anxious, or afraid
at the same time.

ABOUT THE AUTHOR

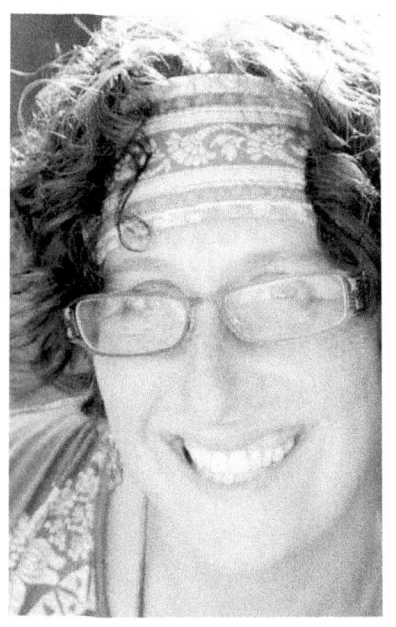

If you enjoyed the inspirational quotes in this book, you also might enjoy Alice's book of inspirational words and poetry called *Read this When…Empowering Messages for Powerless Moments.*

Alice Langholt is the founder and Executive Director of Reiki Awakening Academy School of Intuitive Development (ReikiAwakeningAcademy.com). Her other books include the award winning book, *Practical Reiki: for balance, well-being, and vibrant health. A guide to a simple, revolutionary energy healing method* and *The Practical Reiki Companion* workbook.

Alice is also the author of a series of books, cards, and products for busy people, which focus on 30 second methods of self-care, including: *A Moment for Mom, A Moment for Us, A Moment for Success,* and the A Moment for Me 365 Day Calendar. Find them at amoment4me.com. She has also published a work of fiction entitled *First Family.*

Alice is a wife and mother of four children and lives in the Washington, DC metro area. Visit her author website at AliceLangholt.com.

Did you like this book? Please leave a review on Amazon.com or GoodReads.com.

www.ingramcontent.com/pod-product-compliance
Lightning Source LLC
Chambersburg PA
CBHW080621190526
45169CB00009B/3251